Getting Ahead in a Just-Gettin'-By World

Building Your Resources for a Better Life

DeVol, Philip E.
    Getting Ahead in a Just-Gettin'-By World: Building Your Resources for a Better Life. viii, 138 pp.
        Bibliography pp. 133-137
        ISBN 1-929229-28-3

1. Education   2. Sociology   3. Conduct of life   4. Title

Illustrations by Jayson Grigsby.
Caricature by Mario Luque.

We gratefully acknowledge the mental model used on p. 83 which is adapted from the work of Mentoring Our Moms for Success at the Gault Family Learning Center in Wooster, Ohio.

Other titles

Bridges Out of Poverty: Strategies for Professionals and Communities
    Ruby K. Payne, Ph.D., Philip DeVol, Terie Dreussi Smith

A Framework for Understanding Poverty
    Ruby K. Payne, Ph.D.

Philip E. DeVol

Getting Ahead in a Just-Gettin'-By World

Building Your Resources for a Better Life

ACKNOWLEDGMENTS

Getting Ahead in a Just-Gettin'-By World: Building Your Resources for a Better Life is built on the work and ideas of Dr. Ruby K. Payne. Her description of the hidden rules of economic class is so accurate, so insightful, that people from all backgrounds experience "aha" moments of insight when they hear her speak or read her writings. I recognize that Ruby has given me a fine gift and a huge responsibility by allowing me to present her ideas to people who are living in poverty. It is her innovative approach that makes this workbook unique.

From the time I began working with Ruby and with Terie Dreussi Smith on *Bridges Out of Poverty: Strategies for Professionals and Communities,* I wondered how Ruby's information could be shared directly with people in poverty. It took awhile and a couple of false starts but, thanks to writers and thinkers in a wide variety of disciplines, including people living in poverty, the ideas finally evolved.

I want to thank the folks in Mount Vernon, Ohio, who met with me at The Harbor for so many weeks while we explored ways to utilize Ruby's concepts. I hope you are happy with the final product. The door to everything that happened there was opened by Gloria Parsisson and Diana Williams of the Knox County Department of Job and Family Services. Thank you for taking a chance on me and the groups who met at The Harbor.

Thanks also to the group in Minneapolis who tested the workbook. You will recognize your input and the changes you recommended. Jodi Pfarr, also of Minneapolis, talked theory, philosophy, and down-to-earth reality with me. Thank you for the intellectual honesty, as well as your energy.

My wife, Susan, patiently read and commented on several drafts. The best way I could thank her was to stop writing and send it away to our real copy editor, Dan Shenk. I'm grateful to Dan for scouring my prose and doing all the other chores that copy editors do, raising the quality of writing in the process, and most importantly, forcing me to clarify my thinking. Thanks to Frieda Probst whose careful design work has gone so far in making the workbook appealing and easy to use. I'm sure I speak for all of us when I thank Peggy Conrad, representing **aha!** Process, for her smooth, kind, and competent style of management.

TABLE OF CONTENTS

MODULE 1

Getting Started

INTRODUCTION

Getting Ahead in a Just-Gettin'-By World is for people on the lower rungs of the economic ladder. It is about building economic stability. People who want to can use *Getting Ahead* to build their own path to a good-paying job, to stable housing, and to the ability to save for a rainy day and old age.

In *Getting Ahead* we study economic classes to better understand how the economy works. This workbook is not about social class. Social class is about judgment, comparison, and snobbery – and takes place in all economic classes. In our book, once people are squared away economically, it's simply their choice what they drive, what they wear, or the music they dance to.

The goal of *Getting Ahead* is to help you create your own path for making a stable, secure life for you and your family. In moving through this workbook, you aren't going to be handed a plan and told to follow certain steps. We know that all people have their own story, and everyone is different. For that reason, it's important that each person create his/her own plan. We're all living out the stories of our lives. Part of that story comes from our past, from where and how we live, from the people in our lives, from history, and from world or national events. Who we are today was decided by what we did yesterday; who we'll be tomorrow is decided by what we do today. Whether we know it or not, we're all creating our future stories right now. You can use *Getting Ahead* to help create your future story.

Frank, Ruby, and Tom Payne
Baytown, Texas

This work is based on Ruby Payne's ideas. It is her framework for understanding economic class that shows us how to improve our situations and our communities. Ruby's ideas are helping thousands of kids from poverty do better in school and thousands of workers do better on the job.

Ruby Payne, Terie Dreussi Smith, and I wrote *Bridges Out of Poverty* in the late '90s for people who work in social service agencies, healthcare industries, the criminal justice system, mental health and substance abuse treatment agencies, and community development. At first we spent most of our time presenting these ideas to people who worked in agencies. Now it's time to also share these ideas with people who are living toward the bottom of the economic ladder.

Susan and Phil DeVol
Marengo, Ohio

USING *Getting Ahead in a Just-Gettin'-By World*

Co-Investigating: The person heading your workgroup has been trained as a facilitator and co-investigator. When acting as a facilitator he or she will be making sure things run smoothly and that group members get through the workbook. As a co-investigator, he or she will be working with you (the other co-investigator) to uncover and explore new information. We can all learn from each other and we can all help dig up the information we need.

There will be lots of talk but very little lecturing. People learn in different ways so we will vary the exercises we use for presenting information. We'll also try to be flexible about how we cover the information. If we need to take more time in one area and less in another, we can do that, no problem.

What we will be learning and why: It's important that you know what will be covered, why it's important, and how the information fits together. At the beginning of each module or section you'll see a table that explains exactly that. Here is the table for this section:

Learning Objectives

WHAT'S COVERED	WHY IT'S IMPORTANT	HOW IT'S CONNECTED TO YOU
You will:	This module lets you know what to expect from Getting Ahead and the group.	Each module will begin with a table like this to help you see where you've been and where you are going. The information and ideas build as we go.
Meet everyone in the group.		
Learn about co-investigating.	If the sessions have a pattern or structure to them, it makes it safer to learn and investigate.	
Learn how the workshop will work using the Process Triangle.		
Find out about your pay and what's expected of you.	One pattern that you will see a lot is planning. Each session will begin with planning to give us practice at making a list of what must be done and making sure that everything gets done.	
Make and agree on the rules for the group.		

THE 'HOW IT WORKS' TRIANGLE

The triangle you see below is a symbol or mental model that includes, in capsule form, everything we'll be doing. It describes how we can change our lives – how we can use *Getting Ahead* and the plans we create to build economic security for ourselves. The triangle will appear at the beginning of each module to show us which section we're working on. Once you've learned what each section of the triangle means it will be a quick and easy way to tell us where we've been, where we're going, and how it all fits together. To understand what we'll be doing, we'll start at the bottom of the triangle and work our way to the top.

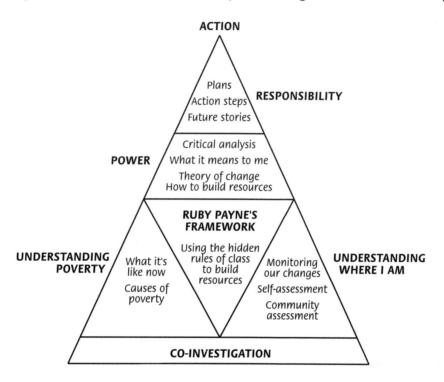

BOTTOM OF THE TRIANGLE: CO-INVESTIGATION

Co-investigation is the foundation of the triangle. This means that everyone in the group is a co-investigator. Together, the group will investigate every part of the triangle. For example, sometimes the group will study big issues that affect all people in poverty, and at other times the investigation will be into our own lives. The point is ... everyone has something to offer, and everyone is a problem solver.

BOTTOM LEFT SIDE OF THE TRIANGLE: UNDERSTANDING POVERTY

In these modules we'll nail down exactly what it means to live in poverty.

MODULE 2: We'll investigate poverty, how it works in the lives of people at the bottom of the ladder, and how it works for us individually. We'll make a mental model (or drawing) of "What It's Like Now."

MODULE 4: To understand poverty, we have to study the full range of research that's done on economic issues. This section spells out the whole story. We'll learn that poverty is not just about the choices that poor people make. We want the plans we make to be broad enough to cover all the causes of poverty.

CENTER OF THE TRIANGLE: RUBY PAYNE'S 'FRAMEWORK'

This is the centerpiece of our work. When we understand how the different economic classes work, we'll be able to figure out what we need and how to get it. We'll use the hidden rules of economic class to build our resources.

MODULE 5: The wealthy, the middle class, and the poor ... each group has its own hidden rules. If we decide we want to get out of poverty, we've got to know and be able to use the hidden rules of middle class.

MODULE 6: If we're going to build economic security, we've got to know exactly which resources we have to improve. This isn't just about money; it's about all aspects of our life. This module defines the resources.

BOTTOM RIGHT SIDE OF THE TRIANGLE: UNDERSTANDING WHERE I AM

Now that we've investigated poverty and learned what Ruby Payne has to say, it's time to apply the information to ourselves.

MODULE 7: If we're going to do something to build economic stability, we're certainly going to have to change some things we're now doing. Whatever plans we make, they should be ours and not someone else's. This module shows us how we can take charge of our changes, and it gives us a way to check on how we're doing.

MODULE 8: Most of the agencies we go to evaluate or assess us in some way. A self-assessment is even more important because we can include everything, not just one part of our lives, and we do it, not someone else.

MODULE 10: In this module, we complete the work we began in MODULE 4 by doing an assessment of community resources. This will lead to our plan for community prosperity.

CENTER SECTION: POWER

In this section we think about the meaning of everything we have learned. When we see the big picture we can do a critical analysis and figure out what it means to us and what we have to do about our situations. With the information we have, we can gain power in our own lives and in our communities.

MODULE 3: When we go to the agencies and government for help, we find that we're expected to change and to make plans. The question is ... whose plan for change is it? Is it ours? Will the plan help us get out of poverty? The theory of change, or the idea behind this workbook, is that we must take charge of our own lives.

MODULE 9: Building resources is the only way to establish economic stability, but it's hard to do. If it were easy, we wouldn't be getting together to do this. The thinking we do here will be used when we make our individual plans.

TOP RIGHT SIDE OF THE TRIANGLE: RESPONSIBILITY

People who have power are people who look for solutions. Now it's time for us to take responsibility for finding solutions in our lives. In these modules we make our personal plans for moving from poverty to prosperity.

MODULE 11: Here is where we work together to build individual plans for gaining economic stability. We'll be creating our future stories.

MODULE 12: We also can be problem solvers in our community and contribute to the fight against poverty and for prosperity. Our voices must be heard.

TOP OF THE TRIANGLE: ACTION

Getting Ahead is designed to bring you right up to the point of action. This is when you take your knowledge, insights, and plans and put them to work

NOTE: MODULES 1 and 13-15 are not included in the triangle because they aren't related to the theory of change. They cover the introduction (MODULE 1), the closing (MODULE 13), and resources (MODULES 14 and 15).

PAYMENTS

You will get paid to investigate this information and develop plans for how you and your community can fight poverty. The amount you'll be paid will be determined by the budget of the organization sponsoring this workshop.

TAKING PART

We know that everyone has experiences, skills, and talents that can be used to help others and the community, so we need you to share your ideas, thoughts, and feelings with the group.

MAKING IT COMFORTABLE

Sometimes it's hard to talk in a group, so we have to make it safe for ourselves. Here are some ground rules that should help. Your group can add to these or change the wording – whatever works for you and the group.

1. No putdowns, violence, or threats of violence.
2. One person at a time talks.
3. Show respect for each other by listening carefully.
4. What's said here stays here, unless someone specifically says something can be shared more widely.
5. No giving advice.
6. Respect differences.

ROOMS, SPACE, AND LEARNING STYLES

This isn't school, so don't make it look like one. Sitting around a table or in a circle gives everyone equal space and encourages conversation. People learn in different ways, so lectures won't be used much. Instead, discussions, stories, drawing, and doing things will be the main ways we learn. Sometimes all we need is a little information to get the picture. We'll spend about half of the time coming to understand the problems and half on strategies for dealing with the problems.

START EACH SESSION WITH PLANNING

We're going to be flexible, so we won't know exactly how much of each session will get done in the time we have. That means each session has to start with planning what we expect to do in that session.

MAKING A LIST OF PROBLEMS

Sometimes so much is happening in each of our lives that we have to talk about it. Sometimes so much is happening that we could talk about it for the whole session. So … someone needs to write down the problems that people are having. The problem list will grow as the sessions go along. At the end of our time together, we'll have a list of problems faced by low-income people that can be shared with people who design and run programs in the community.

PERSONAL AND PRIVATE PROBLEMS

If something personal comes up that might interfere with your ability to participate in the group, ask to meet with the facilitator privately.

AT THE END OF EACH SESSION …

Go over what has been done and see how close you came to following the plan that was set up at the beginning of the session. Make a note about where to start the next session.

MAKING A LIST OF THINGS YOU WANT TO DO

Along the way you may think of all sorts of things you think need to happen in the community or in your life. We'll be developing plans for the things that need to change, so we suggest that you write down your ideas as they come to you in the sections marked **REFLECTIONS** that you'll find throughout this workbook.

What It's Like Now

Learning Objectives

WHAT'S COVERED

You will:

Learn what mental models are.

Investigate what it's like to live in poverty.

Make a "Life in Poverty" mental model.

Figure out your debt-to-income ratio.

Investigate income and wage information.

Make a "What It's Like Now" mental model of your life.

WHY IT'S IMPORTANT

It's important to start with what is REAL. To do that we have to listen to each other and ask tough questions. All that you do in *Getting Ahead* is based on having a true picture of what your life is like.

It's also important that we begin to investigate community issues that foster poverty, such as housing and wages, because poverty isn't just about the choices an individual makes.

Almost every agency you go to will have a plan for you. Going through this workbook is the first step in creating your own plan.

HOW IT'S CONNECTED TO YOU

These are the first mental models that you will create. We will use mental models throughout the workbook.

The "What It's Like Now" mental model will show you where you are. In order to be able to make changes, you need to know where you are now.

It's important to understand how much you need to earn an hour to have financial stability.

BACKGROUND INFORMATION

We've used the words "mental model" several times already. Now we need to define what we mean because we'll be using mental models from here on out. As the facilitator shares this information, listen for the key words and write them in the blanks.

Mental models are _____, _____,

_____, and _____,

Mental models are helpful because they _____, _____,

_____, _____, and _____ .

> *Mental models can change our view of reality.*
> *They show us the big picture.*

INFORMATION

The whole group is going to investigate and describe what life is like for someone living in poverty. If we're going to do something about being in poverty, we had better know exactly what we're talking about.

Activity: Making a pie chart showing all the parts of life in poverty
Time: 30 minutes
Materials: Flip chart, marker
Procedure: 1) On the top of the page write: "Life in Poverty."
            2) Draw a big circle on the page; it should just about fill the page.
            3) As the group discusses life in poverty, draw in and label the pieces of the pie.

        Questions to get started:
        • What problems does a person in poverty have to solve?
        • What do people worry about?
        • Where does most time and energy go?

        Note: Keep this mental model. You may need to add things to it later.

DISCUSSION

1. What did we learn from this investigation?
2. What is it like to live in poverty?
3. What are the biggest problems for people in poverty?
4. What problems take the most time and energy to deal with?
5. Is poverty the same for everyone? How is it different? How is it the same?
6. Do you think that middle-class and wealthy people know what it's like to live in poverty? What kinds of things do you think they know? What kinds of things don't they know?
7. If middle-class and wealthy people did this exercise, what do you think their mental model would look like? How do they spend their time? What do they worry about?
8. How hard is it to get out of poverty? Why?
9. What happens to someone who lives in poverty for a long time?
10. Who needs to see the mental model of poverty that we just did?

REFLECTIONS REFLECTIONS **REFLECTIONS** REFLECTIONS REFLECTIONS
*Write or draw your personal thoughts in the space below. What did you learn from this?
How does it apply to you? What conclusions have you come to about poverty in America?
What conclusions have you come to about where you are now?*

INFORMATION

Now that we've done the "Life in Poverty" mental model for most people in poverty, we need to do the same thing for each of us. Everyone has his/her own story; all our situations are different. If we want to do something about our own life, we'll need to examine it as carefully as we can and do a "What It's Like Now" mental model of our life.

When we did the "Life in Poverty" mental model, we talked about housing and jobs in a general way. Now we need to really investigate housing and wage issues in detail.

The lack of affordable housing is one of the engines that drive chaos and insecurity. Some people in poverty are in subsidized housing; others are on their own to find a solution. This means that people are returning to live with relatives or are crowding into apartments, houses, and trailers with friends. People are living in campgrounds, long-term motels, cars, shelters, and on the street.

Exactly how serious is the housing problem for you? One way to tell is to use middle-class methods of calculating how much of your income goes for housing. When a person goes to a bank for a loan, the banker calculates the debt-to-income ratio to see if the borrower can afford to buy the house. Let's investigate our own debt-to-income ratio.

ACTIVITY

Activity: Calculating your debt-to-income ratio
Time: 20 minutes
Materials: Calculator
Procedure: Write your answers on the worksheet below. See the example.

Example ...

1. How much is your monthly rent or house payment?	$400
2. How much do you owe in car payments per month?	$100
3. How much do you pay on credit cards per month?	$50
4. How much do you pay for loans, payday lenders, lease/purchase per month?	$50
5. How much do you pay for renters/home insurance per month?	-0-
TOTAL DEBT: ITEMS 1-5	**$600**
6. How much gross income (before taxes and deductions) do you have per month?	$800
7. How much do you get in food stamps per month?	$50
8. How much child support do you get each month?	$200
TOTAL INCOME: ITEMS 6-8	**$1,050**
Divide your DEBT by your INCOME. This is your DEBT-TO-INCOME RATIO.	**57.14** **57%**

1. How much is your monthly rent or house payment?	
2. How much do you owe in car payments per month?	
3. How much do you pay on credit cards per month?	
4. How much do you pay for loans, payday lenders, lease/purchase per month?	
5. How much do you pay for renters/home insurance per month?	
TOTAL DEBT: ITEMS 1-5	
6. How much gross income (before taxes and deductions) do you receive per month?	
7. How much do you get in food stamps per month?	
8. How much child support do you get each month?	
TOTAL INCOME: ITEMS 6-8	
Divide your DEBT by your INCOME. This is your DEBT-TO-INCOME RATIO.	

Question: When a person goes to the bank for a loan to buy a house, what debt-to-income ratio is recommended?

Answer: 25-30%. The debt-to-income ratio should not be over 40%. The higher the number, the worse it is. Why? Because the more you spend on housing, the less you have for food, transportation, medical expenses, and the other necessities of life.

DISCUSSION

1. What debt-to-income ratios did members of the group have?
2. What is the quality of housing? Is it safe? Are repairs being made?
3. Is housing affordable?
4. How far do people have to go to find a good job?

MORE INFORMATION ON HOUSING

To continue our investigation on housing, consider these facts:

1. Fifty-nine percent of poor renters spend more than 50% of their income on shelter (Dreier, Peter. Summer 2000. "Why America's Workers Can't Pay the Rent." *Dissent*. pp. 38-44).

2. In 1970 there were 7.3 million low-income families and 9.7 million low-income rental units. In 1985 there were 11.6 million low-income families and 7.9 million low-income rental units (Mattera, Philip. 1990. *Prosperity Lost*. Reading, MA. Addison-Wesley. pp. 128-129).

3. In 1991 there were 47 affordable rental units for every 100 low-income families. In 1997 there were 36 affordable rental units for every 100 low-income families ("Rental Housing Assistance – The Worsening Crisis: A Report to Congress on Worst-Case Housing Needs." March 2000. Housing and Urban Development Department).

DISCUSSION

1. What conclusions can you draw from these facts?
2. What is the trend in housing opportunities for low-income families?
3. How does your housing situation get in the way of having a stable economic life?
4. How do housing conditions affect children? How safe are crowded situations? Can children get a good night's sleep?

REFLECTIONS **REFLECTIONS** **REFLECTIONS** REFLECTIONS REFLECTIONS
*Use the space below to write or draw your ideas and insights
on the housing situation for you – or for people in poverty in general.*

INFORMATION

Now we're going to investigate the relationship between housing costs and wages. The questions we need to answer are: "How much do we have to make an hour to afford the rent? And how much is left over for the rest of your expenses?" Remember, your debt-to-income ratio should be no more than 40%.

Activity: Calculating the hourly wage needed to pay the rent and have enough money left over to meet your other expenses

Time: 15 minutes

Materials: None

Procedure: 1) On the chart below find the hourly wage that is closest to what you are earning now or the hourly wage you earned at your last job. Circle that dollar amount.

2) On the row where you found the hourly wage look at column 5 to see what the cost of rent would be at 35% and 50%.

3) Next, in column 5 find the dollar amount closest to what your rent is now *in the 35% rows only and see what hourly wage you would need to be making to afford the rent.*

4) Read the examples below.

5) Investigate with the group the meaning of this information.

1 Hourly wage	2 Hours worked per month	3 Monthly income	4 Percentage of income for rent	5 Cost of rent	6 Money available for other expenses	7 How much money is left over for other expenses when you pay 35% instead of 50% of your income for rent
$ 6.00	173	1,038	35%	363	675	156
	173	1,038	50%	519	519	
$ 7.00	173	1,211	35%	424	787	181
	173	1,211	50%	606	606	
$ 8.00	173	1,384	35%	484	900	208
	173	1,384	50%	692	692	
$ 9.00	173	1,557	35%	545	1,012	233
	173	1,557	50%	779	779	
$10.00	173	1,730	35%	606	1,125	260
	173	1,730	50%	865	865	
$11.00	173	1,903	35%	666	1,237	285
	173	1,903	50%	952	952	
$12.00	173	2,076	35%	727	1,349	311
	173	2,076	50%	1,038	1,038	

Adapted from the work of Glenn Corless, Columbiana County (Ohio) One Stop

Example of how to read the table: *If John worked eight hours a day, five days a week, he would be working an average of 173 hours a month. If he earned $6 an hour and his rent was 35% of his income, he would be paying $363 for rent and would have $675 left over for other expenses. If John paid 50% of his income on rent, he would be paying $519 for rent and have only $519 left over for other expenses. When paying rent at 35% John would have an extra $156 to spend on other expenses.*

Example 2: *Sally is single with no children. She makes $11 an hour and should be paying $666 or less for rent, but she is currently paying $800. Paying $666 for rent she would have $1,237 for other expenses, $134 more than she has now.*

DISCUSSION

1. What are the "other" expenses mentioned in columns 6 and 7 that people have?
2. If Sally wanted to move to a less expensive place, what problems might she face?
3. How would Sally's situation change if she had children?
4. Discuss some ways that people can balance the wage/rent issue in the short term. How do people solve this problem?
5. If someone is making low wages and paying more than 35% of his/her income on housing, what will be the long-term effect on the children?
6. Discuss some ways that people can solve the wage/rent problem in the long term.

To continue our investigation, answer the questions below. They are designed to help apply this information to your story. You will use this thinking to fill in the "What It's Like Now" mental model.

What is the hourly wage at your current job?_____

How much did you get paid at your last job?_____

What was the most you were ever paid? _____

How long did you have the best-paying job?_____

What's minimum wage in your state?_____

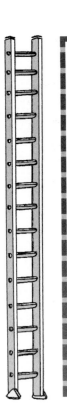

Homework

INVESTIGATE THIS!

- What is a living wage?
- How much do you think a person has to make per hour to have decent housing, pay for utilities and insurance, purchase clothing, go to a movie once a month, eat out in a modest restaurant once a month, buy healthy food (but not real expensive cuts of meat), and put a little money into a savings account each month?
- How many cities and counties in the United States have passed a Living Wage Ordinance?
- How is a living wage calculated?

Where might you go to learn more about this? Is there someone in the group willing to start this investigation?

DISCUSSION

1. What have you learned from this investigation?
2. If a person on welfare were to do everything his/her caseworker told him/her to do, got a job, and kept it for a year, at the end of that year would he/she be any closer to getting out of poverty?
3. Is it possible for a person to have a full-time job and still be in poverty?
4. In your community, what do employers pay new employees?
5. How does the hourly wage affect housing?
6. How does housing affect jobs?

ACTIVITY

Now it's time to create our own mental models for "What It's Like Now." This is a picture of each of our lives at this time. We've investigated only two pieces of the pie (housing and wages); there are many more. Your group may choose to co-investigate other aspects of your life, such as health or transportation, in the same way we investigated housing and wages.

Activity: Creating your personal "What It's Like Now" mental model
Time: 15 minutes
Material: Work space on the following page

Procedure: 1) Draw a large circle that covers most of the available space below.

2) Using a pencil (because you may want to change things as you go), draw in the pieces of the pie for every part of your life and label them.

3) Make each piece of the pie large or small according to how important it is.

DISCUSSION

1. What is the largest piece of your pie? Why?

2. How hard is it to break out of the circle?

3. What makes it hard to make changes? Come up with a list of the reasons why it's hard to break out of the circle.

4. What did you learn about poverty by doing this mental model?

5. What did you learn about yourself by doing this mental model?

6. What did you learn about your community or "the system" by doing this mental model?

*In the space below, write or draw your personal thoughts
about your "What It's Like Now" mental model.
Have you thought about your life like this before?
Is your thinking about poverty starting to change?*

REFLECTIONS REFLECTIONS REFLECTIONS REFLECTIONS REFLECTIONS REFLECTIONS

NEW NEW NEW NEW NEW VOCABULARY NEW NEW NEW NEW NEW

Words   Meanings

_____   _____

_____   _____

_____   _____

_____   _____

_____   _____

_____   _____

_____   _____

_____   _____

Theory of Change

Power		
	ACTION	
	Plans **RESPONSIBILITY**	
	Action steps	
	Critical analysis	
	What it means to me	
	Theory of change	
	How to build resources	
	RUBY PAYNE'S FRAMEWORK	
UNDERSTANDING POVERTY	What it's like now / Using the hidden rules of class to build resources / Monitoring our changes	**UNDERSTANDING WHERE I AM**
	Causes of poverty / Self-assessment	
	Community assessment	
	CO-INVESTIGATION	

Learning Objectives

WHAT'S COVERED

You will:

Examine which agencies require clients to change.

Investigate how plans are made in agency settings.

Explore ways that people change.

Study changes that you have made.

Learn the theory of change for *Getting Ahead.*

WHY IT'S IMPORTANT

Learning about change is important because to get out of poverty you will have to do things differently in order to change.

Agencies have some of the resources that you may need, so you'll probably have to work with them, at least for a while. Middle-class organizations are all about change.

Getting Ahead is based on a theory of change that we need to share with you.

HOW IT'S CONNECTED TO YOU

The problem is poverty and how it affects you.

If you want to get out of poverty you'll need to be in charge of the investigation, the plans, the action, and the monitoring.

INFORMATION

It's time to investigate how change and plans are handled by the agencies we go to. This investigation can best be done by the group.

Activity: Examining agency approaches to change

Time: 30 minutes

Materials: Flip chart

Procedure:
1) Make a list on the flip chart of the agencies and programs that group members go to. Some examples might be substance abuse treatment programs, mental health clinics, homeless shelters, probation/parole offices, welfare-to-work agencies, and schools.

2) On the "Life in Poverty" mental model that you created as a group, draw a line pointing to a piece of the pie and write on that line the name of the agency that is meant to help in that area. For example, Metropolitan Housing would be written on a line outside the circle pointing at the piece of the pie marked "housing."

3) Mark an "X" beside the name of the agency that requires you to make changes in the way you think or behave.

4) Mark a second "X" by those agencies that suggest plans for how you should change. Sometimes these plans are called by different names, such as reunification plans, treatment plans, contracts, or commitments.

5) Which agencies require or ask you to create plans for the changes that you will make?

The "Life in Poverty" mental model now looks different because the pie is surrounded by names of agencies.

DISCUSSION

1. Are there any parts of the pie where there is no agency or organization with a mission to assist people in that area?

2. Do most agencies ask for change in the client's life? About what percentage of the agencies require planning?

3. Do agency plans cover your whole life or just a piece of the pie?

4. What do you feel when you look at the agencies surrounding the "Life in Poverty" mental model?

5. What have your "change" experiences been like with agencies? Has your life changed much as a result of going to an agency?

6. Do you think it would be better to make your own plans, taking into account the entire picture? Why or why not?

7. Why is change by the client so important to people who work at agencies?

INFORMATION

Almost all agencies and organizations that serve the poor are about change – the changes that they believe clients need to make. Agencies, like people, have what is called a "righting reflex." When they see something that isn't right, they usually have an idea on how to make it better.

For most people, the righting reflex works like this: You're watching TV, and you can't locate the remote. You eventually find it in the other room, and your righting reflex is, "Hey, you kids! I've told you a thousand times to leave the remote on the coffee table!" The righting reflex also works in deeper ways, because inside all of us is that place where we know what's right, and we want to do it. It's an internal guide or "compass."

So ... the righting reflex is basically a good thing, something we all have and need. And yet, there can be problems with the righting reflex. The first is when we don't take charge of our own life and make our own plans for righting things that have gone wrong. The second is when the agencies impose their plans without taking the client's complete situation into account.

Some people hate change. They never want to change, they don't want things to change, and they don't want others to change. But even those who hate change ... change. Other folks are good at changing; they do it smoothly. And then there's everyone in-between. There are some things about living in poverty that make it harder to make changes. Richard Farson, author of *Management of the Absurd* (1997), noticed that the more resources a person has, the easier it is for him/her to change. In other words, the fewer resources a person has, the harder it is to change.

Hundreds of books and articles have been written on change; some are even worth reading. We don't have time to go into them here, but check the reading list in MODULE 15 for titles we recommend.

If you want to figure out an agency's theory of change, look carefully at what the agency workers have you do while you're with them. Keep track of what happens step by step as you work through the program ...

- What do you learn about?
- Do you work on personal issues?
- Do you make a plan to change your behavior?
- Do you meet in groups or individually with a counselor?
- What kinds of support do you get?
- How do the agency workers measure the changes you make?

Below are just a few of the approaches that agencies take to change, minus the 64-dollar words.

1. If we give you accurate information – in other words, educate you – then you should be able to use the information to change.

2. If we provide support (transportation, childcare, etc.) and remove other barriers that keep you from participating, then you will be able to use the information to change.

3. If we design the program so that you can participate, then you should be able to use the information to change.

4. If we raise your awareness about the benefits of a change, then you'll become motivated to try new behaviors.

5. If it's painful or you feel personally threatened by the problem, then you'll be willing to change.

6. If the benefits outweigh the costs, and if you believe that you have the skills to change, then you'll be able to change.

7. If you are held accountable for your choices and behaviors, then you will change.

ACTIVITY

Activity: Deciding to change
Time: 15 minutes
Materials: Flip chart
Procedure: 1) As a group, add more theories of change to the above list.

2) Discuss which strategies have been used on you and which strategies you've used on others. Which strategies "worked" for you – and which ones didn't? Why?

3) List and discuss reasons why poverty makes it hard to change.

4) Think of times when you have changed and when you've seen others change for the better. List and discuss the factors that made it work.

ACTIVITY

Think of a time when you made a change. This should be a time when it was a conscious choice, not something that someone else controlled, but that you did out of your own motivation. For example, it could be that you broke up with someone, took a class, or quit smoking.

Now, *answer these questions:*

1. What was different about the way you thought about the experience of change that made it work?
2. Did you follow the example of someone else who had been successful in making a change?
3. Did you learn by watching the mistakes made by someone else?
4. Did you repeat a pattern or strategy that you had used before?
5. What new ideas or information did you have that made it easier to change?

In the space below, write out any thoughts and ideas that in the future will help you change.

INFORMATION

When we take Ruby Payne's information to people who work in agencies, we encourage them to spell out for their clients exactly what their theory of change is and to provide a mental model that describes that theory of change. It's only right that we do the same – to tell you what our theory of change is for *Getting Ahead* and the group that you're in now.

It's important that you understand this theory of change because you will be asked to follow steps and prepare a plan of action for yourself. At this point, we aren't asking for a commitment – just an open mind.

GETTING AHEAD's THEORY OF CHANGE FOR GETTING OUT OF POVERTY

- Living in poverty makes it hard for people to change. The "What It's Like Now" experience is a trap that forces many people to live in the moment *and* in chaos.
- Because of this, it's especially important that people in poverty come to understand the big picture about poverty, to learn that poverty is about more than the choices they make.
- It's also important to learn how poverty impacts individuals. That means learning about the hidden rules of economic class, resources, family structure, and language issues is crucial to doing a critical analysis of the situation.
- When people in poverty understand the big picture, as well as their own issues, they will know what to do.
- Doing an assessment of both personal resources and community resources will allow an individual to make his/her own plans for economic stability.
- Using the hidden rules of economic class to build resources will ease the transition to stability.
- Partnerships with the middle class and other people will build vital social support.
- Working on individual plans is not enough because poverty is a systems problem too. Plans also must be made to address community problems.
- People in poverty are problem solvers.

The Process Triangle that was introduced earlier is a mental model for change in this workbook.

MODULE 4

The Rich/Poor Gap and How It Works

Understanding Poverty

ACTION

Plans
Action steps
Future stories — RESPONSIBILITY

Critical analysis
What it means to me
Theory of change
...to build resources

What it's like now
Causes of poverty

PAYNE'S FRAMEWORK
...hidden class

Monitoring our changes
Self-assessment
Community assessment

UNDERSTANDING WHERE I AM

UNDERSTANDING PO...

CO-INVESTIGATION

Learning Objectives

WHAT'S COVERED

You will:

Understand the causes of poverty.

Review the four categories of poverty research.

Establish that there is a need for strategies to reduce poverty from all four areas of research.

Investigate the rich/poor gap and learn how it works.

Establish a strategy to protect yourself from predators – defined as people and businesses that profit by taking advantage of people in poverty.

Make mental models for what life is like for people in middle class and wealth.

Introduce the concept of sustainability.

WHY IT'S IMPORTANT

It's important to know how the economic system works so we can do good thinking about what hurts and helps those people who are at the bottom of the economic ladder.

It's important to know that poverty is not just about the choices of the poor. Community and system issues also must be addressed.

We need to see the abstract, the big picture, before we can make good decisions. There's an important connection between seeing the abstract and making good decisions.

HOW IT'S CONNECTED TO YOU

We established the reality of living in poverty when we made the "What It's Like Now" mental model.

Now we are establishing the other realities about poverty and comparing them with what life is like for people in middle class and wealth.

We need to have a plan for ourselves and our community's political/economic system if we're going to build economic stability and sustainability.

INFORMATION

Much research has been done on poverty in this country – in fact, so much that there's actually a research industry just on poverty. Poverty has been studied from every angle by all sorts of groups: universities, governmental organizations, foundations, institutes, and think tanks. And then there are the groups and individuals who comment on the research and use it to set policy. Those groups focus on one type of research or another and often bend it to their purpose. So ... governmental policy and anti-poverty programs do not come directly from pure research. There are very good reasons why people in poverty should know about poverty research and comment on it. That's what we're going to do now.

Activity: *Causes of poverty*
Time: *15 minutes*
Materials: *Flip chart*
Procedure: 1)   *Using the space below, write a list of the things that you think cause poverty. Keep this list to look at later.*

2)   *Have a volunteer make a list of the group answers to the following question: What do most people say causes poverty?*

FOUR AREAS OF RESEARCH

The facilitator will share information on four areas of poverty research. Fill in the left column with topics that are studied and the right column with strategies that are designed to "fix" each problem.

No. 1: Behaviors of Individuals in Poverty	
Research Topics	**Strategies**

No. 2: Human Skills and Social Systems	
Research Topics	**Strategies**

No. 3: Colonial Exploitation	
Research Topics	**Strategies**

No. 4: Political/Economic Structures	
Research Topics	**Strategies**

DISCUSSION

1. While looking at the list of causes of poverty that the group made earlier, mark each "cause" with a 1, 2, 3, or 4 (above) for the area of research it fits in.
2. Which category got the most hits? Why?
3. Which category got the least? Why?
4. Which of these categories of research do welfare reform programs fit into?
5. What does this mean to people who are using the programs?
6. What are people in poverty being told about themselves by society and the programs it offers?
7. Does your community provide a full range of strategies for dealing with poverty? What does your community do well in this area – and what does it not do so well?

SOME CONCLUSIONS ABOUT THE RESEARCH

- There is valid research in each of the four categories.
- There are causes of poverty in all four categories, so there must be strategies for all four.
- Poverty isn't just about the choices made by the poor; there are many causes of poverty that the poor can do nothing about.

REFLECTIONS **REFLECTIONS** **REFLECTIONS** REFLECTIONS REFLECTIONS
*In the space below, write or draw your thoughts and feelings about the causes of poverty.
In what ways do you think differently about your situation now?*

ACTIVITY

Activity: Making a list of predators
Time: 10 minutes, or homework
Materials: Worksheet
Procedure: We need to examine in detail how predators impact each of our lives. (See the first box in this module for a definition of predator in this context.) It isn't enough to say they're out there; we've got to figure out just how entangled we are with them, investigate how they work, and help each other get out from under their control.

1) As a group, list all the predators you can think of in your community.

2) On the worksheet below, make a list of predators.

3) Privately, not as a group exercise, mark an "X" in the middle column for every predator you have some association with.

4) As a group, list what a person has to do to get out from under the control of a predator.

5) Privately, write down a quick plan for what you can do about each predator whom you marked with an "X."

6) If you have some connection with a predator, go back to your "What It's Like Now" mental model and add each predator.

PREDATORS

List the predators in your community. Are you associated in some way with this predator? If so, how? How can someone get out from under a predator's control? How long might it take?

Predators		
List the predators in your community.	Are you associated in some way with this predator? If so, how?	How can someone get out from under a predator's control? How long might it take?

DISCUSSION

1. What do I need that has caused me to become associated with a predator?

2. Was there ever a time when you didn't have to relate to predators? When was that? What were your circumstances at that time?

3. What would it be like for you if you didn't need to have any involvement with predators?

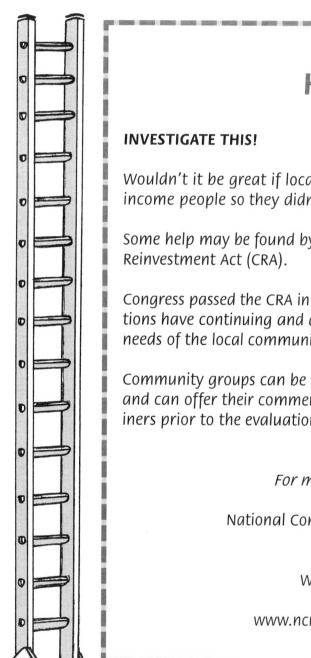

Homework

INVESTIGATE THIS!

Wouldn't it be great if local banks would provide fair loans to low-income people so they didn't have to go to predators?

Some help may be found by learning how to use the Community Reinvestment Act (CRA).

Congress passed the CRA in 1977. It states that "regulated financial institutions have continuing and affirmative obligations to help meet the credit needs of the local communities in which they are chartered."

Community groups can be involved in the plans developed by local banks and can offer their comments on the CRA performance of banks to examiners prior to the evaluation of the bank.

For more information contact:

National Community Reinvestment Coalition
Suite 540
733 15th St., NW
Washington, DC 20005
(202) 628-8866
www.ncrc.org/cra/how2usecra.html

In the space below, write or draw your ideas and feelings about predators.

INFORMATION: THE RICH/POOR GAP – ECONOMIC DISPARITY

The gap between the rich and poor in the United States has been getting wider since the late 1960s, but hardly anybody (except some economists and social activists) has paid much attention. People in poverty are too busy stamping out fires in their struggle to survive to pay attention. Most of the middle class is too busy trying to climb the economic ladder to look beyond the next rung. And the people who benefit from this structure the most, the wealthy, don't even want to talk about it.

It's time to talk about it. Here are some themes you'll want to explore in detail.

In America for the past 30-40 years, the rich (top 10%) have been getting richer, and the poor (90%) have been getting poorer. This is the fourth time in American history that the gap has widened in a statistically significant way. The first was in the Gilded Age, the 1870s; the second was during the Roaring Twenties; the third was the Nifty Fifties; and the most recent growing divide was fueled by the "bull markets" of the '80s and '90s.

Let's investigate how the wealth gap works.

The following information is provided by United for a Fair Economy (UFE). Quoting from UFE, "Whenever possible, [UFE] uses government sources, such as the U.S. Census Bureau (e.g., family income), the Federal Reserve Bank (e.g., household wealth), and the Bureau of Labor Statistics, etc. Even with their well-documented flaws, government statistics are generally the most comprehensive, frequently updated, and widely cited."

ACTIVITY

Activity: 1979 to 2001 real family income growth by quintile and top 5%
Time: 15 minutes
Materials: Five income placards
Procedure: 1) Review the tables on the following page.

2) Group investigates the information presented by the facilitator and five volunteers.

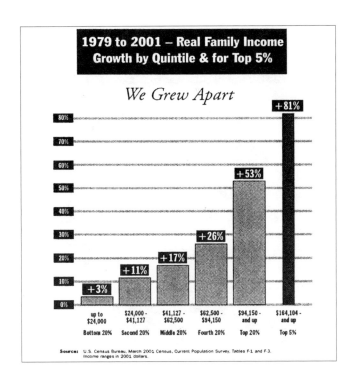

1979 to 2001 – Real Family Income Growth by Quintile & for Top 5%

We Grew Apart

Source: U.S. Census Bureau, March 2001 Census, Current Population Survey, Tables F-1 and F-3. Income ranges in 2001 dollars.

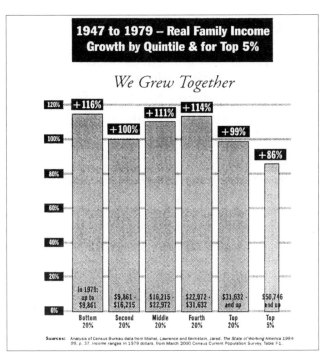

1947 to 1979 – Real Family Income Growth by Quintile & for Top 5%

We Grew Together

Sources: Analysis of Census Bureau data from Mishel, Lawrence and Bernstein, Jared. *The State of Working America 1994-95*, p. 37. Income ranges in 1979 dollars. from March 2000 Census Current Population Survey, Table F-1.

ACTIVITY

Activity:	CEO pay as a multiple of average worker pay, 1960-2000
Time:	15 minutes
Materials:	Six placards
Procedure:	1) Review the table at right.
	2) Group investigates the information presented by the facilitator and six volunteers.

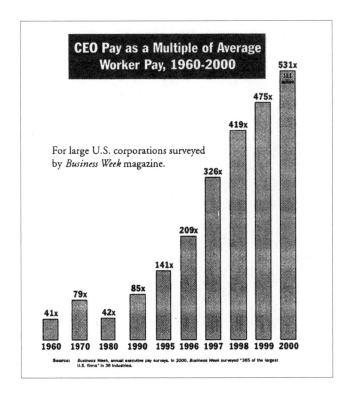

CEO Pay as a Multiple of Average Worker Pay, 1960-2000

For large U.S. corporations surveyed by *Business Week* magazine.

Source: *Business Week*, annual executive pay surveys. In 2000, *Business Week* surveyed "365 of the largest U.S. firms" in 36 industries.

ACTIVITY

Activity: Ownership of household wealth in the United States: "The Ten Chairs – the Difference Between Wealth and Income"

Time: 10 minutes

Materials: 10 chairs

Procedure:
1) Review the charts at right.
2) Group investigates the information presented by the facilitator and the 10 volunteers.

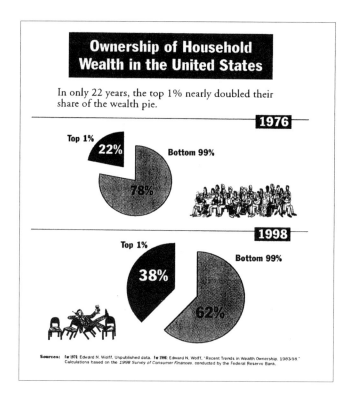

ACTIVITY

Activity: Individual tax collections vs. corporate tax collections

Time: 10 minutes

Materials: None

Procedure: Review the table at right and discuss the meaning of the information.

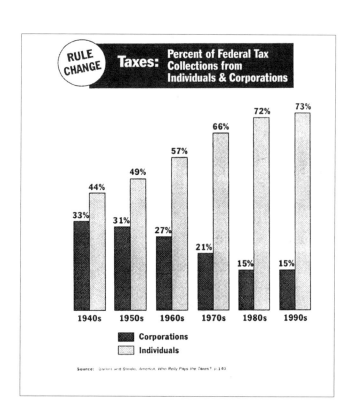

- *Definitions*
  - Individual federal tax collections include individual income tax, Social Security, and Medicare taxes.
  - The chart does not include excise taxes (such as the tax on phone services, gasoline, and airline tickets) or tariffs (taxes on imports), which is why the percentages do not add up to 100.
- The share of federal revenue being raised by corporate income tax has been declining since the 1950s in the United States. This is the result of lower rates and more loopholes.
- As a result, the individual share has grown. In recent years the wealthiest individuals are escaping the higher tax rates of a few decades ago, and a greater burden has been shifted onto lower-income and middle-class people.
- The personal exemption used to be a much higher percentage of people's income. The falling real value of the personal exemption has hurt low- and middle-income taxpayers.

WHO PAYS THE MOST TAXES? WHAT'S THE BREAKDOWN?

So now we know that corporations are paying less tax and individuals are paying more, but which individuals pay the most? The U.S. Internal Revenue Service figures show that the top 10% of households (measured by income) pay 70% of all federal taxes. The bottom 50% of households pay 4% of taxes. This contribution to federal (and state) taxes is important to the long-term stability of the community. When a community loses high-paying jobs because of business closings or relocations, or the people with those jobs move to better school districts and safer developments, their contributions to the community are lost.

PUTTING ALL THESE IDEAS TOGETHER: DEVELOPING SUSTAINABILITY

In this module we've reviewed the causes of poverty, examined economic disparity, looked at who pays the most taxes, and learned what it means when the group that pays the most taxes leaves the community. The next question is what happens to a town, city, or county where this pattern of economic instability exists? What does this mean to our children and to their children? Can this pattern go on the way it is and provide a decent life for them?

Making a stable life for ourselves *and* future generations is called sustainability. Creating sustainability may well be the biggest issue facing our generation. The first major revolution that our human ancestors faced was moving from a hunter-gatherer way of life to farming – or an agricultural economy. It required people to develop new knowledge and skills, to build permanent homes, to store food, and to organize communities in new ways. The second revolution was the change from farming to industry, often called the Industrial Revolution (of the 1700s and 1800s). Again, new skills, knowledge, and tools were used to spur development. The third revolution is the information/technology development of the last 20-25 years. Two things – intellectual capital and virtually instantaneous information flow – are relatively new realities that are changing the face of economies, societies, and cultures worldwide. The fourth revolution is the development of sustainability. The questions we must answer are: How can we use the earth's resources and yet have enough for future generations – and how do we live in the environment and yet maintain it for our children?

These questions may not seem very important to someone living in survival mode. After all, if you can't find an affordable or safe place to live, are you going to be worrying about the problems of future generations? Not likely, but here's the thing. According to Thomas Sowell, a historical and international demographer, none of our towns, cities, or counties can develop a sustainable future if they allow any group to be disenfranchised or left out for any reason (economic class, race, religion, etc.) because the whole community will become economically poorer. Take poverty, for example. When the percentage of people in poverty reaches 35 to 40%, the community becomes alarmed, and when it reaches 60%, most of the top 10% move out. Is that a sustainable trend? Will our children be better off or worse off if this pattern continues?

Obviously political/economic issues and sustainability are very complex, and in the days to come all economic groups and communities will have to struggle with them. If we get confused by all the details of complex issues, we can refocus ourselves by coming back to the big-picture questions of sustainability.

- Will future generations of all groups live well if this trend continues?
- Will the decisions we are making (whatever they are) create long-term economic stability for all groups into future generations?

Creating sustainability is something all economic groups will have to pay attention to because we're all in this together. For that reason, all three economic groups will need to cooperate and *work* together.

ACTIVITY

In order to understand the impact of economic disparity (the rich-poor gap) on people at the lower end of the economic system, we created a mental model of poverty. Now we need to create mental models of middle class and new money/old money so that we also understand how these people live, think, and make decisions. After all, no single economic group is responsible for causing poverty, and no single economic group can create sustainability.

Activity: Read the descriptions below and as a group draw a mental model of middle class and a mental model of wealth.

Time: 75 minutes

Materials: Flip chart and markers

Procedure: 1) Read the description of middle class and draw a mental model.

2) Read the description of new money and old money and draw a mental model.

3) Review the mental model of poverty that was done in Module 2.

4) Make a list of the things that appear in middle class, new money, and old money that do not appear in poverty.

5) Make a list of things that appear in poverty but do not appear in middle class and wealth.

Middle Class

Mark and Mary were both raised in middle-class families. Mark's father worked in a steel mill and belonged to a union. His mother ran the house and was active in the community. Mary's father was an accountant, her mother a teacher. Mary went to college for one year. Mark was in the military for two years. They are in their early 40s and live in an established but sinking neighborhood in a mid-sized city. This is the second marriage for both of them. They have two children, a 15-year-old daughter from Mary's first marriage and an 11-year-old son they had together.

Mark works for a light manufacturing company making $15 an hour, or about $32,000 a year. Mary works for a state agency where she earns $8.50 an hour, or about $17,680 a year. They have excellent health care benefits but worry that their employers will shift more of the cost to the employees. Rumors are circulating that Mark's employer will be relocating to Mexico or China. Mark is worried because he doesn't have knowledge-sector skills. He has begun to think about going to school, but he's not sure what he would like to do. Mary's job isn't much more secure because budget problems at the state level are resulting in layoffs.

Mark and Mary bought their cars new. Mary drives a mini-van; Mark drives a truck. They bought their house on a 25-year mortgage 12 years ago. Just recently they took out a second 20-year mortgage to remodel the kitchen and bathroom, re-carpet the house, and consolidate some consumer loans. Now that their house is fixed up they plan to sell it. Their neighborhood has been changing, and they want to sell before property values drop any lower. They want to get their kids into a safer and better school. Moving to a development and into a bigger house will strain their resources. Saving money for the kids to go to college seems impossible.

Their children are very busy too. Their daughter has been in dance and singing classes from the time she was little, and now she's on the volleyball and swimming teams. Mark coached his son's PeeWee team; Mark and his son enjoy playing golf together. The boy is in his school's chess club and Boy Scouts.

Thanksgiving, Christmas, and other holidays have to be scheduled very carefully because their daughter goes to her father's house. Mark's parents live close by so the family sees them regularly. The only time they see aunts, uncles, and cousins are at Thanksgiving and a summer picnic. The highlight of the year is the annual camping trip in the summer. The family enjoys making plans to explore different parts of the United States. Mark and Mary like camping because not only do the kids get to see the attractions and historical sites, but they learn to be responsible to each other. The children like it because they get to swim, canoe, ride bikes and horses, and visit parks.

Mark is a member of the Moose where he and Mary eat once a week. Mary and her friends go shopping together and like home decorating. She goes to the YWCA to exercise and is active in the PTA at their son's school.

New Money

Nathan and Nancy are in the new-money class. They started their own company 10 years ago and are now multi-millionaires. Nathan was raised in extreme poverty, and Nancy came from middle class. They have been married 20 years. The first 10 years of their marriage money was very tight. They lived very simply in a two-bedroom house because Nathan wasn't making very much money, their son was small, and they were living on Nancy's salary as a nurse. Nathan had a variety of jobs selling cars and insurance, along with work in the construction industry. He also worked as a stockbroker for a time. Things changed dramatically when Nancy wrote a book about nursing the elderly that became a hit. She self-published, and she and Nathan started a publishing company. Within five years they were millionaires.

Nancy and Nathan's company grew so fast they had to work very long hours on the business, and they had to work hard to learn how to run a company. Their accountant told them, "The money from the business is not yours. Don't ever make the mistake of thinking it is. Give yourself a small salary and do not take funds out of the company. That is not your money." Because Nancy and Nathan trusted the accountant, they did what he said. So the first year there was no extra money for anything but the business.

When they first started the company, Nancy and Nathan would get up at 2 a.m. to do the paperwork and fill book orders, then work all day at their regular jobs. Nancy kept her job for a year; Nathan kept his for four years. They were both tired. and they fought a lot. They ran the business out of their home, sharing the space with a part-time employee and buying new equipment to keep up with the growing work. They needed a regular office but couldn't afford it right away; instead they bought a bigger house with space over the garage for the office, but Nathan hated the lack of privacy because by now they had one full-time person and one part-time person working for them. At the end of the first year, the accountant said to take the extra money and put it into savings. Forty percent of that extra money went to the Internal Revenue Service.

As the business grew, they had more to learn. For example, they learned that after a person makes $250,000 a year he/she loses all deductions, house interest, etc., so Nathan and Nancy paid off the loan on their house. On another occasion electronic tax deposits were not made on time, and their company was fined $4,000 by the IRS. Recently, the tax bill from IRS was for more than $1 million. The accountant told Nancy and Nathan that if they were willing to move money twice between two accounts, they could save $2,500 on their tax bill. They chose not to do it because the last time they tried it money got lost in the transfer, and it took hours of time, multiple phone calls, and three weeks before the accounts were straightened out.

Nancy and Nathan realized that they couldn't keep track of everything. The investment counselor told Nancy that some of the investment money needed to be moved. But Nathan, who had worked in the board of trade and knew how shaky those money deals could be, said no to the idea. Nancy understood that their money was not making money for them the way it should, but neither of them had enough time to work on it. In addition, the last investment counselor they had took all the profits that they earned in making trades, so they actually made less money. Nancy knows that the bank balances can vary as much as a $100,000 a month. Keeping track of what goes on requires that she has people she can trust.

The growing business meant more employees and more lessons to be learned. One night Nathan got a call from Brinks that the security alarm had gone off at one of the buildings. Nathan could have handled the problem easily if the custodian had not turned off the cell phone and if the Brinks people hadn't given them the wrong security code in the first place. Instead he spent an hour explaining who he was to the police while trying to calm the custodian who hated the police. Nancy and Nathan gave a bonus to their employees because it was very important to them that employees be treated well. It was an ethical issue for Nathan and Nancy. So

continued on page 39

New Money *continued from page 38*

at Christmas the hourly wage employees got a $3,000 bonus.

The growing business also meant making new and sometimes uncomfortable choices. Nancy traveled a lot speaking about her book; her appearance was important. Recently she started having a tailor make her clothes. She knew that only a few people in the audience cared about her clothes, but those few people were the ones who control the budgets. Nancy knew that her appearance could sometimes make or break a deal and that she could never predict when that might happen, so she now wears tailored suits all the time. One suit costs $2,500, a price that was hard for Nancy to accept. She calls it an "occupational hazard."

There are now 40 part- and full-time employees who

depend on her for work and their income. Nancy works at setting the company goals and making sure things work well.

In their personal life Nathan and Nancy have a lot going on too. Ida, their longtime housekeeper, is getting ready to retire, and Nancy and Nathan worry about her. They gave her a salary and set up a retirement account for her. Ida's children constantly borrow money from her, and she buys food for her grandchildren. Nathan helped her negotiate a wonderful price on a new car on which she makes payments. Nathan re-roofed and re-sided her house and put in new windows as a gift to her. Nathan and Nancy are working on how to help Ida retire gracefully with enough money.

Nathan's brother often gets drunk and drives without a

license; his license has been suspended in two states. Nathan does what he can to look after his brother, checking to see if he's OK when he doesn't show up for work. On one occasion Nathan went to the emergency room at 2 a.m. to get his brother who was drunk and cussing at the staff. Nathan is the only one who can handle his brother when he's drunk.

Nancy and Nathan are putting their son through college, as well as one niece. Nancy's mother asked that they pay the college tuition for yet another niece. Nancy would like to have more friends, but the business takes just about all of her and Nathan's time. Because Nancy travels so much, it is hard to have social activities. She considers a quiet evening at home a wonderful thing.

Old Money

Olen is 24 years old and in generational wealth, also known as old money. His grandfather made the original fortune in the shipbuilding industry, and both of his parents were raised in wealth. A trust fund was established at his birth, but he also was named in other trusts as "future progeny," so he has several trust funds. He was registered for private boarding school at birth. At 6 years of age he went to boarding school. He graduated from Yale University, as did his father. At 21 Olen began receiving a monthly check from the interest in his trust

fund, but he won't control the principal until he's 35. Twice a year he meets with two people: his trust adviser, who happens to be his father, and his lawyer to be updated on his trust fund.

Olen spends a great deal of time in social activities; only up to a point does he use his social and financial connections to further his career as a playwright. Olen is a bit unusual for his social group in that he wants to be an acclaimed writer. He knows he can be published; he has enough connections to do that, but he wants to be respected and renowned in his own right. It

is expected that by 30 years of age he will join one of the family businesses.

Olen's hobbies are sailing, golf, ballooning, flying (his own plane), skiing, and the theater. He spends part of the year in Palm Springs, California, part of the year in Colorado (Aspen and Vail), part of the year in Europe, and part of the year in New York City. In addition, he travels either first class or, more often, in the corporate or family jet. He has domestic help who take care of everything: his clothing, the cleaning, the meals, etc. A tailor makes

continued on page 40

his clothes and often selects both fabric and style, as the tailor knows Olen's personal tastes. In fact, at one of the family estates one person is hired full time to take care of the pool area and another to polish the brass. Because there is always staff around, privacy becomes a huge issue. Staff members are fired for not being discreet.

In the garage are several cars and vehicles. Rather than try to manage all the different keys, all the vehicles have been keyed to one key so a last-minute choice of cars can be made.

Olen's allowance is $10,000 a month. He doesn't have bills because he lives in one of the family homes or apartments around the world and doesn't pay for the utilities, grounds-keeping, etc. Additionally, two residences were given to him as gifts. His private club memberships are paid for by the family, and one of his cars was a gift at college graduation. He has no debt. His trust is managed by the family accounting and law firm.

Right now, however, he is involved in a lawsuit against his own family. His father divorced his mother when he was 10 years old and married a much younger woman. His father now has two children by his new wife. When his father and mother divorced it was an ugly battle, and a separate trust fund was established for Olen.

A few years ago, when Olen was having lunch with his father, his dad made an off-the-cuff comment that made Olen suspicious. So he hired an attorney to investigate the status of his trust fund that his father was to be overseeing. What Olen found was that an elaborate "paper game" had been created. Olen's trusts, which were to have assets of $1 billion, had assets of only $180 million.

The legal situation is very complex, but in short the family has about 100 trusts, several of which are offshore and overseas and were established before the Internal Revenue Service closed the loopholes. Consequently, these trusts were "grandfathered" into the law and don't have to conform to current laws. What Olen's father did was establish many trusts, then set up banks to house the money from the trusts. His father started new businesses whose primary funding came from the bank, which got its money from the trusts. Olen's trusts had provided a great deal of money for businesses that weren't making money, so his original trusts weren't being reimbursed for the money that was taken out of them. Furthermore, Olen found out that his father had "gifted" $200 million to his current wife's mother that had never been reimbursed. (The $200 million was a loan that was never paid back, i.e., it became a gift. It was written off as a bad debt.)

Olen started the lawsuit against his father when he turned 21; it has been going on for three years now. Olen is seeking to have the original money reinstated to his trust and to control his own trust. He knows it will be a protracted struggle because his father once waged a 20-year battle against the IRS over what the IRS said was insufficient payments.

Some of Olen's club memberships have been pulled. In other words, he must pay the club fees himself. During his parents' divorce proceedings, his mother was wise and got several lifetime memberships for Olen. The part Olen doesn't like is that the lawsuit has been discussed and examined in such publications as the *New York Times, BusinessWeek,* and *Forbes.* Several of his own family members no longer speak to him. Olen expects to be mostly alone by the time the fight is finished. But he's determined to win, and he knows the fight will get even uglier before it's over.

Olen spends most of his time with old-money friends like himself or friends from the theater. He doesn't need to worry that they will make fun of him for his tastes in clothes or art. He has learned to be very careful and guards his privacy closely. Since the legal fight with the family started, he has gotten, by court order, a bodyguard to be paid for directly from his trust. Furthermore, he doesn't take phone calls. All calls are forwarded to the lawyer handling the lawsuit against his father.

DISCUSSION

1. Does this information on the economy change your thinking or feelings about poverty?
2. Where do you think your knowledge of the economy and poverty come from?
3. What might be the effect on your life if you continued to think in the ways you did before?
4. If you were to go farther into this new thinking, how might that affect your future?
5. What is likely to happen if the community does nothing differently?
6. What kinds of things could people in the middle class and poverty do together?
7. What are some things that people from all three classes can do to make a more stable community – to develop sustainability?

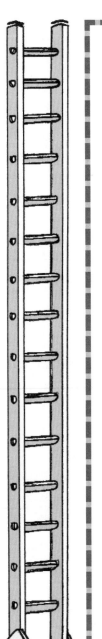

Be a Community Problem Solver

INVESTIGATE THESE WAYS TO HELP CREATE COMMUNITY STABILITY!

UNITED FOR A FAIR ECONOMY
United for a Fair Economy (UFE) is looking for volunteers to teach its manual, *The Growing Divide: Inequality and the Roots of Economic Insecurity*. The exercises we just did came from that manual. UFE supports many strategies for creating economic stability in the United States. When recruiting trainers, they say, "Imagine that in several years there are 10,000 of you traveling the city streets and country lanes across the U.S. inspiring people to take action."

United for a Fair Economy
37 Temple Place, Second Floor
Boston, MA 02111
(617) 423-2148
(800) 564-6833
www.ufenet.org

If teaching a class is not for you, consider some other options. Your skills, gifts, and talents might match up best with some other group or organization, such as:

NEIGHBORHOOD WATCH
PARENT/TEACHER ASSOCATION OR ORGANIZATION
VOLUNTEER FIRE DEPARTMENT
RED CROSS VOLUNTEER
CRISIS PHONE CENTER
SCOUTING
4-H ADVISER

In the space below, write or draw your ideas and thoughts about economic differences.

REFLECTIONS REFLECTIONS REFLECTIONS REFLECTIONS REFLECTIONS

NEW NEW NEW NEW NEW VOCABULARY NEW NEW NEW NEW NEW

Words	Meanings

MODULE 5

Hidden Rules of Economic Class

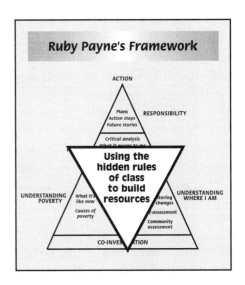

Ruby Payne's Framework

ACTION

Plans
Action steps
Future stories

RESPONSIBILITY

Critical analysis
What it means to me

Using the hidden rules of class to build resources

UNDERSTANDING POVERTY

What it's like now

Causes of poverty

Monitoring changes

Self-assessment

Community assessment

UNDERSTANDING WHERE I AM

CO-INVESTIGATION

Learning Objectives

WHAT'S COVERED

You will:

Understand the key points to remember while learning about the hidden rules of economic class.

Explore the hidden rules and apply them to yourself.

Explore language registers and find out why there are so many misunderstandings between and among the classes.

Investigate language experience and learn how to help children succeed in school.

Examine family structures and learn about the impact of poverty on families.

Examine the patterns of behavior that come out of the family structure.

Learn how and when to use the hidden rules to help you in your situation.

Learn how to do mediation (a way to build thinking structures) with your children.

WHY IT'S IMPORTANT

This information is *abstract,* not concrete, and yet it's important to know this so that we'll have new ideas on how to solve problems.

Knowing this information can help us develop economic security.

HOW IT'S CONNECTED TO YOU

Earlier we found that poverty is about being stuck in the tyranny of the moment.

In the "Theory of Change" module, we learned that we need abstract information to give us options.

This information is the heart of what Ruby Payne has to share with us. Our job is to first learn it, then get good at using it in our everyday life.

This module is packed with ideas. There's a lot to explore here, so it will take more than one session to get through it.

INFORMATION

In this module we begin to explore and learn Ruby Payne's ideas on poverty and economic class. Her work is very different from others who have written about poverty. Most studies focus on race and gender when describing poverty. Ruby Payne's long-term study of a low-income neighborhood offers a new way to understand the impact of poverty that "clicks" with those who hear it, especially with those live in poverty or grew up in poverty.

The key points below are the foundation for everything else we're going to cover. They describe our approach to poverty and this work – what we're trying to do and what we're not doing.

KEY POINTS TO REMEMBER

1. Poverty is relative.
2. Poverty occurs in all races and in all countries.
3. Economic class is a continuous line, not a clear-cut distinction.
4. Generational poverty and situational poverty are different.
5. This work is based on patterns. All patterns have exceptions.
6. Working on poverty issues without dealing with race, ethnicity, gender, and other cultural issues is impossible. This work, however, focuses on economic class alone.
7. An individual brings with him/her the hidden rules of the class in which he/she was raised.
8. Schools and businesses operate from middle-class norms and use the hidden rules of middle class.
9. Understanding the hidden rules of economic class allows a person to choose behaviors that lead to economic security.
10. In order to move from poverty to middle class or middle class to wealth, an individual must give up relationships for achievement (at least for a period of time).
11. No matter what economic class we're in, we try to earn the respect of the people closest to us.
12. We cannot blame the victims of poverty for being in poverty. We cannot support stereotypes and prejudices about the poor.
13. There are many reasons for poverty; we must have a wide array of strategies to end poverty.

Review and discuss these key points before moving on.

INFORMATION: DEFINING THE HIDDEN RULES OF ECONOMIC CLASS

Hidden rules can be about belonging. How do you know when you belong? When you don't have to explain anything you say or do to the people around you. To fit in like that you have to know the unwritten and unspoken cues and habits of the group. When you know the hidden rules, you don't have to worry about being understood. Wherever we go we're surrounded by hidden rules because all groups of people and all cultures have their own hidden rules. We have hidden rules for nationality, neighborhoods, clubs, gangs, race, age, gender, ethnicity, history, the workplace, and, yes, economic class.

Think about the different sets of hidden rules that the following individuals might have:

- A young black man recently from Somalia, now living in Columbus, Ohio (with others from Somalia), who doesn't speak English well, has a middle school education and is working at a grocery store stocking shelves.
- A middle-aged black woman with a career in hospital administration, living in Baltimore, married to a teacher, raising teenage sons.
- An old, white woman living in a small town in Iowa, recently widowed, active in church and senior citizen activities, supported in part by her four children.
- A young, Hispanic man living in L.A., a college graduate, starting a career in social work, recently married with a baby on the way.
- A young, white woman living in rural Indiana, with three children, a high school education, a part-time job at a discount store, supported in part by welfare, with a boyfriend who is in jail.

All these people have hidden rules of culture, history, and economic class.

1. What sets of hidden rules do these people have?
2. Could any of them share hidden rules?
3. Who are the hidden rules hidden from?
4. How do we learn the hidden rules we use?
5. How can we learn the hidden rules of another group?

SUGGESTIONS ON HOW TO STUDY THE HIDDEN RULES

Before we get into the hidden rules, here are some ideas to help you get everything you can out of them.

- We will be studying the hidden rules of economic class only. Middle-class people of all racial and ethnic groups share some economic class rules; the same is true for people in poverty and wealth. We are not studying other sets of rules.

- Understanding the hidden rules of economic class can help you *if* you don't think of them as *right* and *wrong, good* and *bad* – as if you have to be *for* or *against* them. It's more helpful to think of them as "rules" that children learn almost unconsciously when they're growing up. Naturally, they will use them in their own life.

- Understanding the hidden rules can help you *if* you don't think of them as your *identity.* If you cling to your hidden rules as a description of who you are, it will be very hard to use them to help yourself and others.

- Think of the hidden rules as a *choice* or as the *rules of a game.* The more rules you know, the more games and sports you can play. For example, if you want to play basketball, you have to know the rules. You can't play poker if you don't know the rules. So ... if you want to do well at work and school, you'll need to know and use middle-class rules. That doesn't mean the rules of poverty are wrong. Use the rules of each class when and where you need to. One woman who is a supervisor in a government organization said, "When I'm at work I use the middle-class rules. When I'm at home with my friends, I use the poverty rules."

- Understanding the hidden rules can help you *if* you don't use them to judge others or to compare yourself with others.

- Judgments and comparisons happen in all classes. We tend to watch how we're doing compared with our neighbors and friends. However, that's all about snobbery. People caught up in constant comparisons live on the "knife's edge" between envy and contempt. Instead of snobbery, we prefer to think in terms of economic class. This is about having economic security, something we wish for everyone.

- Breaking hidden rules: It's pretty easy to break hidden rules of the other classes, especially when you're doing new things and meeting people from the other classes. You know when you've broken a hidden rule when the other person suddenly gets quiet, avoids you, or gives you a funny look – the kind of look, as Ruby Payne says, after "something is seen moving in a wastebasket."

- Unfortunately, people get into conflicts over the hidden rules all the time. One of the best things about Dr. Payne's work is that she helps us understand where the conflicts come from. Once we know that there are hot spots, we can choose to handle ourselves differently. Try to get good at noticing and naming the conflicts as they happen.

Here's an example of a hidden-rule conflict: In the first hidden rule, Driving Force (next page), you will learn that, for the middle class, the driving force tends to be work and achievement, and for people in poverty, it is survival, relationships, and entertainment.

One conflict that arises out of this is the judgmental attitude of many middle-class people toward the big-screen TVs and satellite dishes that many poor people own. It's often expressed like this: "I can't believe he has a big-screen TV! He should be using that money to pay his bills." This attitude shows little understanding of what life is like for people toward the bottom of the economic ladder. Learning the hidden rules of class gives this middle-class person a choice about his/her attitude.

USE THIS PATTERN FOR STUDYING THE HIDDEN RULES

We suggest that you use the same pattern for studying each of the hidden rules.

1. **Information:** First, make sure you understand them. Investigate why the rules make sense for each class.
2. **Activity:** Find examples of when you have seen the rules being used by others. Using the forms provided, give examples of how you have seen the hidden rules used.
3. **Discussion:** Discuss what you have learned from this investigation.
4. **Reflections:** Make the information personal to you. Write notes or draw to put your thoughts on paper.

"The Hidden Rules of Economic Class" represents a mental model for how economic class works for or against economic security and stability.

	POVERTY	MIDDLE CLASS	WEALTH
DRIVING FORCE	Survival, relationships, entertainment.	Work, achievement.	Financial, political, social connections.
POWER	Power is linked to respect. Must have the ability to fight. People respond to personal power. There is power in numbers. People in poverty can't stop bad things from happening.	Power is separated out from respect. Must have the ability to negotiate. Power is linked to taking responsibility for solutions. People respond to positional power. Power is in institutions. People in middle class run the institutions of the country.	Power is linked to stability. Must have influence, connections. People respond to expertise. Power is information. People in wealth set the direction for business, corporations, and public policy.
TIME	Present most important. Decisions made for the moment based on feelings or personality.	Future most important. Decisions made against future ramifications.	Traditions and history most important. Decisions made partially on basis of tradition and decorum.

HIDDEN RULE	YOUR EXAMPLE

	POVERTY	MIDDLE CLASS	WEALTH
DESTINY	Believes in fate. Cannot do much to mitigate chance.	Believes in choice. Can change future with good choices now.	Noblesse oblige.
WORLD VIEW	Sees world in terms of local setting.	Sees world in terms of national setting.	Sees world in terms of international setting.
LANGUAGE	Casual register. Language is about survival.	Formal register. Language is for negotiation.	Formal register. Language is about networking.

HIDDEN RULE	YOUR EXAMPLE

	POVERTY	MIDDLE CLASS	WEALTH
EDUCATION	Valued and revered as abstract but not as reality.	Crucial for climbing success ladder and making money.	Necessary tradition for making and maintaining connections.
MONEY	To be used, spent.	To be managed.	To be conserved, invested.
FAMILY STRUCTURE	Tends to be matriarchal.	Tends to be patriarchal.	Depends on who has the money.
POSSESSIONS	People.	Things.	One-of-a-kind objects, legacies, pedigrees.

HIDDEN RULE	YOUR EXAMPLE

	POVERTY	MIDDLE CLASS	WEALTH
PERSONALITY	Is for entertainment. Sense of humor is highly valued.	Is for acquisition and stability. Achievement is highly valued.	Is for connections. Financial, political, and social connections are highly valued.
SOCIAL EMPHASIS	Social inclusion for people he/she likes.	Emphasis is on self-governance and self-sufficiency.	Emphasis is on social exclusion.
LOVE	Love and acceptance conditional, based upon whether individual is liked.	Love and acceptance conditional, based largely upon achievement.	Love and acceptance conditional, related to social standing and connections.

HIDDEN RULE	YOUR EXAMPLE

	POVERTY	MIDDLE CLASS	WEALTH
HUMOR	About people and sex.	About situations.	About social faux pas.
FOOD	Key question: Did you have enough? Quantity important.	Key question: Did you like it? Quality important.	Key question: Was it presented well? Presentation important.
CLOTHING	Clothing valued for its individual style and expression of personality.	Clothing valued for its quality and acceptance into norm of middle class. Label important.	Clothing valued for its artistic sense and expression. Designer important.

HIDDEN RULE	YOUR EXAMPLE

LANGUAGE: A HIDDEN RULE IN DETAIL

We are expanding on the hidden rules of language because our use of language can make or break the way we get along with others. There are several layers to this section that build up to a lot of information that can be used to help us and our children.

DISCUSSION

1. What can you tell about someone by the way he/she talks?
2. Have you ever felt judged for the way you talk?
3. Can you tell which economic class a person is in by the way he/she talks?
4. How much do you think success in school is determined by the way a family talks?

INFORMATION

Every language in the world has five registers (Joos, 1967).

REGISTER	EXPLANATION
Frozen	Language that is always the same. For example: Lord's Prayer, wedding vows, etc.
Formal	The standard sentence syntax and word choice of work and school. Has complete sentences and specific word choice.
Consultative	Formal register when used in conversation. Discourse pattern not quite as direct as formal register.
Casual	Language between friends and is characterized by a 400- to 800-word spoken vocabulary. Word choice general and not specific. Conversation dependent on non-verbal assists. Sentence syntax often incomplete.
Intimate	Language between lovers or twins. Language of sexual harassment.

DISCUSSION

1. Which register is better for understanding intentions, social connections, and daily life?
2. Which register is better for ideas, logic, negotiation, and things far removed from daily life?
3. How far can a child go in school and be successful with just casual register?
4. Why do you think people in middle-class institutions like schools, work, and agencies prefer the formal register and the direct discourse pattern? Which hidden rules are behind that?
5. When a person can shift back and forth between the casual and formal register, we call that person "bilingual." Do you know people who are bilingual? Who needs to be bilingual?
6. Service-sector jobs (entry-level jobs in fast-food restaurants, discount stores, gas stations, convenience stores, hotels) require which register?
7. Manufacturing-sector jobs require which register?
8. Knowledge-sector jobs (where you have the skill and can move any place in the country and get a job – nursing, doctor, veterinarian, attorney, teacher, business, and finance) require which register?

DISCOURSE PATTERNS

Another aspect of language is called discourse pattern. This refers to the way a group of people will carry on a conversation. For example, in some groups it is OK if people talk over each other. In other words, before one person is done speaking another begins talking. In other societies, where the rule is to wait for one or two seconds after a person has finished speaking to begin speaking, it would be considered rude to break in or "interrupt."

The discourse pattern for people who use the formal register is very direct. They will typically present the story or information in chronological order – the sequence of how it happened. The speaker will use abstract terms to present ideas and information. These people go directly to the point and say things like, "Let's get down to business."

The pattern looks like this:

"Let's get down to business."

The discourse pattern for people who use the casual register, on the other hand, is often circular. They go around and around before coming to the point and may jump into the story just about anywhere, not necessarily the "beginning." Instead, they may start at the place that is most interesting or funny. This pattern relies on the use of common words and an ability to tell what people mean by the way they move their body or by their tone of voice. Hosts of late-night talk shows often speak in casual register, using body language and reading the social situation, while making conversation with their guests. Circular stories take much longer to tell than stories in the formal-discourse pattern and often rely on others in the group contributing to the story as it is told.

The pattern looks like this:

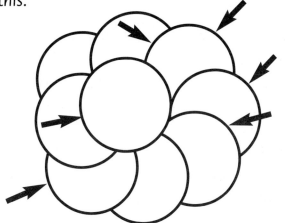

The arrows represent the comments that are added to the story by others as the story unfolds.

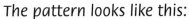

DISCUSSION

1. Which hidden rules are behind the circular story pattern?
2. How do discourse patterns – casual and formal – lead to misunderstandings? Give examples.
3. How would it help someone to know how to use both formal and casual registers?
4. How would it help to be able to use both discourse patterns?

LANGUAGE EXPERIENCE

Most children learn to talk during their first three years, and their experience with language depends almost entirely on their immediate family. The register and discourse pattern of their family will be their register and discourse pattern. Every family has its own culture of talk. Some families talk more than others. Some encourage children to join in the conversation, while others don't.

During the first three years of life, the brain is building pathways for thinking. The more words a child hears from family members, the more pathways are created. The more stories a child hears, the more a family explains how things work, the more pathways are created. Research tells us that children need to hear stories and fairy tales several times a week in order to build thinking pathways.

The typical story pattern in books for children looks like this:

THE FORMAL-REGISTER STORY STRUCTURE STARTS AT THE BEGINNING OF THE STORY AND GOES TO THE END IN A CHRONOLOGICAL OR ACCEPTED NARRATIVE PATTERN. THE MOST IMPORTANT PART OF THE STORY IS THE PLOT.

GOLDILOCKS AND THE THREE BEARS

Remember the story of *Goldilocks and the Three Bears*? Take a minute to talk about the story in the group, then answer these questions.

1. What happened first?
2. When Goldilocks got to the house, she did three things. What were they, and in what order did they happen?
3. Each time she tried something in the bears' home she tried them in a certain order. What was that order?
4. When you read a fairy tale to a child, how does he/she like it when you skip a page or try to change the story?

INFORMATION

The above story pattern is a storage/retrieval system that children use for remembering the information in the story. In their brain they put the porridge first on the "curve" (previous page), the chair second, and the bed last. Putting these items into the thinking pattern of the story allows them to go back to those places to find the details of the story.

There are other patterns – or mental pictures – that children will rely on too. For example, they will recall that each time Goldilocks tries things in the bears' house, it's in this order: "Papa Bear, Mama Bear, and then Baby Bear."

The reason children like to hear the story again and again is to gain mastery over the story. They like and want to be able to anticipate and predict what will happen. This is why children don't like it when adults "mess" with the story by skipping a page or making up different events. So, on behalf of all children, don't mess with the story!

Children need to hear a fairy tale several times a week to embed this thinking mechanism in their brain.

DISCUSSION

1. Notice the difference between the circular story pattern and the fairy tale structure. How much will or won't the circular story structure give children a thinking structure they can use again and again?
2. Imagine youngsters going to their first day of kindergarten, meeting their teacher, spending their day doing things with other kids, and learning the rules of school. How important is it for them to feel like they fit in, like they belong? What part does language play in their feeling of belonging?
3. What do these things have to do with poverty?

LEARNING TO TALK

Betty Hart and Todd Risley studied how children learn to talk. They studied children in professional, working-class, and welfare homes. Researchers went into the homes soon after a child was born and studied the language experience of the child for about $2^1/_2$ years.

The families in the study were all healthy and loving; there was no addiction or mental illness in any of the families, and all the families had stable housing. The researchers collected so much information that it was six years from the time they began entering data in the computer until the reports were available. Hart and Risley published their findings in *Meaningful Differences in the Everyday Experience of Young American Children* (1999).

In all of the homes the children learned to talk, but there was a big difference in language experience and development by economic class. The following findings illustrate the main differences.

Economic class	Number of words children exposed to from ages 6 months to 3 years	Encouragements vs. prohibitions		Working vocabulary
Professional	30 million	5	1	1,200 at 36 months
Working class	20 million	2	1	No information
Welfare	10 million	1	2	900 for adults

1. Number of words that children are exposed to: The research tells us that the more words children hear from their parents (TV doesn't count) in the first three years, the more neuro-pathways are developed in the brain.

2. Encouragements vs. prohibitions: An encouragement is when an adult responds to a child's interest in something and encourages him/her to explore and talk about it. A prohibition is when an adult stops a child with a "be quiet," "shut up," or "don't do that." The more encouragement the child receives, the more words he/she has and the more learning structures are built.

3. Working vocabulary: The more words children learn, the easier and faster they can learn more words. For example, learning the word "bird" can lead to naming different birds, then learning the categories of birds, and perhaps on to discovering the various life patterns of birds.

DISCUSSION

1. Children from poverty typically are two years behind their peers from middle class and wealth – and often aren't ready for school. Could the information above be part of the reason why?

2. Hart and Risley say it's impossible to suddenly make up 20 million words when a child is 4 or 5, but we also know that it isn't "over" for children who come to school with weak language background. Dr. Payne has ways that help child learn quickly; she teaches these techniques to educators. What are some things families can do right away to help their children? Make a list on the flip chart.

MEDIATION: THE WHAT, THE WHY, AND THE HOW

As suggested in the box at the beginning of this module, there is something parents can do to help their children develop learning structures in the brain. It's called mediation, and it means helping someone understand the mental steps involved in learning (sometimes it's called "thinking about thinking"). This idea comes from Reuven Feuerstein, an Israeli educator who gave people the strategies they needed to do well at work and school – or, in other words, to succeed in the abstract world.

When parents are encouraging their children, as we discussed above, they need to give them three steps: the what, the why, and the how. The "what" is when you point out to children the content of their actions or words, the "why" is when you explain the meaning of it, and the "how" is when you suggest alternative strategies or behaviors for them.

Here is how it looks in a table. In this example, a little boy is standing on the seat of an airport shuttle bus, looking out the window. It's late at night, and everyone on the bus is bleary-eyed and tired – except this 4-year-old boy. The dad says:

WHAT	WHY	HOW
"Hey, you're standing up in your seat."	"When the bus takes off, you might fall down."	"So … why don't you kneel down or sit on my lap."

The boy, who obviously was used to his dad talking to him in this way, knelt down on the chair and happily counted the airplanes as the bus moved along.

In this mediation, the father offers the boy a choice: to kneel down or sit on his lap. Given a choice, the little boy was less likely to feel forced to do something and, at the same time, could practice taking responsibility for his choice.

This is much different from another travel experience. In this case another father and 4-year-old boy were in an airplane traveling across the country – a very long flight. The boy was fidgeting, fussing, and asking a lot of questions. The dad says:

WHAT	WHY	HOW
		"Shut up. Be quiet. Settle down. Stop that" (repeated dozens of times over the next several hours).

In mediation, all three steps are necessary to instill thinking structures. If this father had mediated the situation for his son, what might he have said?

In the space below, write your mediation for the little boy on the airplane. Hint: Don't leave out the "why." Without the why, the thinking piece is missing.

WHAT	WHY	HOW

Mediation takes time but, when used frequently and well, kids are easier to manage, and discipline is about learning, not punishment.

ACTIVITY

Working with one other person, pretend that one of you is a child who just sneezed without covering his/her mouth. How would you do a mediation? Write out the three steps, then try them on the sneezer. Now switch and let the other person try his/her mediation on you.

DISCUSSION

1. Many parents do explain the world to their children in this way. We suggest that we all do it more often. Will this be hard to start doing with your kids? Why or why not?

2. What other examples of mediation do you see?

3. Is the mediation strategy used at work? At agencies? In court?

FAMILY STRUCTURE

The family structure seen in poverty is the subject of many debates. The question is: What causes the structure you see below? Notice that there are three men in Jane's life. This is a called a multi-relational, matriarchal structure where the woman is at the center of the family. Many believe that this structure exists because of the morals of the people involved. Our review of the research leads us to believe that generational poverty and an overload of one crisis after another produces this pattern.

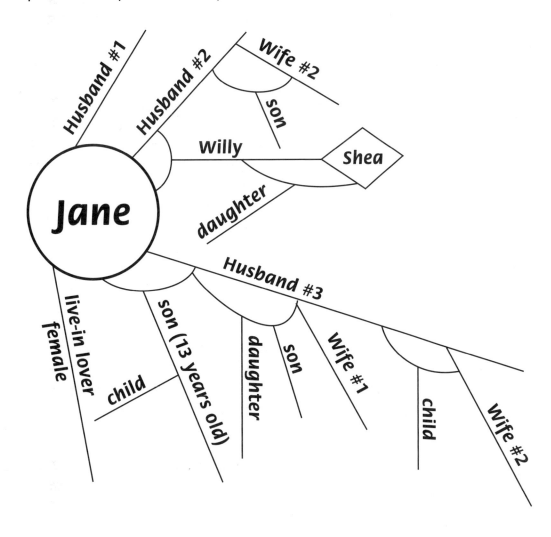

Adapted from A Framework for Understanding Poverty *by Ruby K. Payne*

Families who have economic security typically have the pattern you see on the next page. The "M" stands for marriage; the "D" stands for divorce. Middle-class people change partners too, but they do it in a more "linear" way. When a divorce occurs, the man and woman go through a long legal process to determine who will get what, then they move apart. What drives this structure is the passing on of assets (wealth) either as child support, alimony, or property settlement. For that reason, it's imperative that all the relationships are clearly defined.

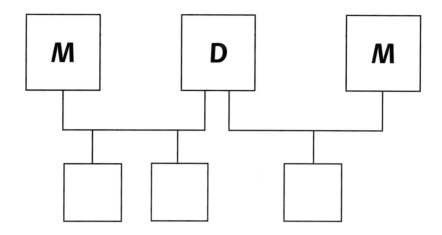

BEHAVIOR PATTERNS THAT COME FROM LIVING IN THE MULTI-RELATIONAL, MATRIARCHAL STRUCTURE

1. **Gender role for men = fighter/lover/protector:** The key issue for males is to be a "man." The rules are rigid, and a man is expected to work hard physically – and be a lover and a fighter. He may come and go a lot and will often be missing from the home. His role is to be a protector, not a provider. Men in poverty do not identify themselves with their jobs.

2. **Gender role for women = rescuer/martyr:** The key issue for females is to take care of and rescue her man and her children. Because the men are often gone, she must manage the family and solve all the problems. Living in the tyranny of survival means that she lives in the high-stress world of endless crises. Men can be a relief to her, and they can addto her problems. There are a number of reasons why a woman in poverty would not want toget married. What are those?

3. **Ownership of people:** People are possessions. The more people you "have" the easier it is to solve problems. There is a lot of fear about family members who may leave the others behind. Remember what we learned earlier: To achieve anything, people in poverty must give up relationships, at least for a time.

4. **Importance of relationships:** Without money to ensure stability, one only has people to rely on. Middle-class people have AAA cards and home insurance to give them security; people in poverty rely on others to fix their car and to live with if they have to move.

5. **Importance of personality:** Being "real" is more important than education, degrees, and accomplishments. Individual personality is what one brings to the house. It's important to be entertaining, to tell stories, and to be funny. One woman told her kids, "We may not have money, but we're loaded with personality."

6. **Mating dance:** In poverty, the mating dance is about using the body in a sexual way and complimenting body parts – both verbally and non-verbally. In the middle class, the mating dance stresses achievements and status at work. Marrying up is a common way out of poverty and a way to learn the hidden rules quickly. On the other hand, people who marry outside their economic classes often find themselves in conflict because of the hidden rules.

7. **Background noise:** When someone is trying to survive, escaping into entertainment is important. The TVs are usually on, no matter what the circumstance. Conversation is participatory, often with more than one person talking at a time.

8. **Lack of order:** The houses and apartments of people in poverty are usually crowded with both people and things. The rooms of the house are used for many purposes – entertainment, eating, and sleeping. There are few organizational devices, such as filing cabinets and planners. Children seldom have a quiet place to do their homework.

9. **Discipline:** Punishment is about penance and forgiveness, not change. Using the diagram below, imagine a man in his 30s who has had a series of service-sector jobs, none of which he keeps very long. He lives with his grandmother who cooks and cleans for him. When he decides he needs a truck to get a job, he gets her to co-sign for him. Before long she's making the truck payments. Later he decides he's going to get married and asks his grandmother for her credit cards so he can get things he needs for the wedding and new apartment. He maxes out her card at $10,000. His grandmother is pushed by other members of the family to kick him out and demand he repay the money. After he's been out for a week, he calls and says that he's living in a car and has no place to live or money to live on, so she takes him back.

The grandson believes that there's nothing he can do beyond or different from what he's already doing, so he takes money from his grandmother. He doesn't want other members of the family to catch him using her money and would make excuses if they found out. When he's finally caught by the others, and they pressure the grandmother to kick him out, he takes his punishment.

What is more important to the grandmother than the truck payments and the $10,000? The relationship with her grandson.

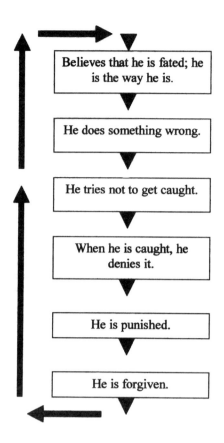

In poverty, the penance/forgiveness cycle is about maintaining relationships and not about changing behavior; it's about the relationship coming back to the way it was. In middle class, discipline is about consequences and change. If you don't change your behavior, you may lose the relationship.

DISCUSSION

1. Someone once said, "No matter what economic class, we all strive to earn the respect of our peers." How might that make it difficult for us to change the way we do things?
2. What is it about poverty and its impact on families that makes it difficult for people to change?
3. Which of the patterns listed on the previous pages causes you problems?
4. Have you seen the penance/forgiveness cycle? Give examples.
5. What happens when someone who is part of the penance/forgiveness cycle gets into trouble with the law or at school?

HIDDEN RULES AND PUBLIC POLICY

Before we leave hidden rules and move on to the next module, let's explore how our knowledge of the hidden rules can help us figure out what is happening at the national policy level. Can we use this information to understand, analyze, and predict the decisions and actions of wealthy and middle-class people?

EXERCISE

1. Draw an arrow from the economic class that creates national anti-poverty and social services policies to the economic class that runs the social service institutions.

2. Draw an arrow from the economic class that runs the social service institutions to the economic class that uses the institutions.

POVERTY	MIDDLE CLASS	WEALTH

DISCUSSION

1. How much influence does the middle class have to shape policies and program designs?

2. How much influence do people in poverty have to shape policies and program designs?

3. Which economic group has the most time and resources to devote to solving problems and pursuing their interests?

4. What are some things that can be done to change this picture?

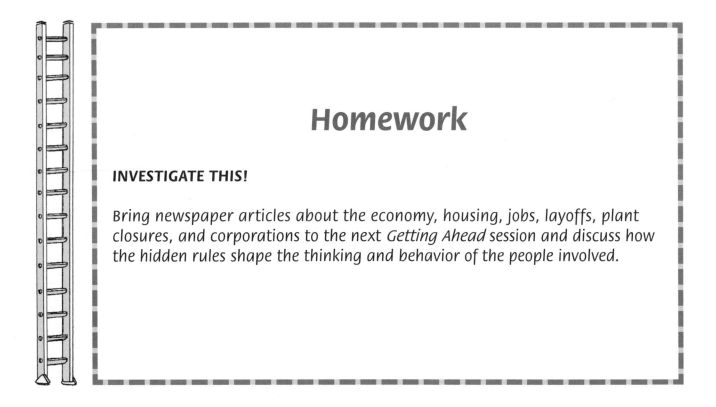

Homework

INVESTIGATE THIS!

Bring newspaper articles about the economy, housing, jobs, layoffs, plant closures, and corporations to the next *Getting Ahead* session and discuss how the hidden rules shape the thinking and behavior of the people involved.

In the space below write or draw your thoughts and ideas on the hidden rules of economic class.
Which rules were you raised with? Which rules do you use now?
Is it important to learn – and sometimes use – rules from other economic groups?
Why or why not?

REFLECTIONS REFLECTIONS REFLECTIONS REFLECTIONS REFLECTIONS REFLECTIONS

Words	Meanings

MODULE 6

Eleven Resources

Ruby Payne's Framework

ACTION

RESPONSIBILITY

Plans
Action steps
Future stories

Critical analysis
What it means to me

Using the hidden rules of class to build resources

UNDERSTANDING POVERTY

What it's like now

Causes of poverty

UNDERSTANDING WHERE I AM

Monitoring changes

Self-assessment

Community assessment

CO-INVESTIGATION

Learning Objectives

WHAT'S COVERED

You will:

Define the resources.

Create your own "social capital" mental model.

Create your own "support for change" mental model.

Use case studies to practice doing assessments of resources.

Explore ways to use this information.

WHY IT'S IMPORTANT

Resources are important because it is by building our resources that we can have economic security.

If we want a rich life in all areas, we need to build other resources.

Investigating our resources leads naturally to ideas for improving our life.

HOW IT'S CONNECTED TO YOU

The hidden rules describe why we behave the way we do.

The resources describe all areas of our life. When we're good at analyzing resources we'll be ready to do a self-assessment of our own resources, then begin making our plans.

INFORMATION: DEFINING OUR RESOURCES

There are 11 resources that everyone needs in order to live well. These resources include financial, emotional, social, and spiritual support. Ruby Payne defines poverty as how much a person does without resources. Obviously, money is one of the resources. When people don't have enough money to meet their basic needs, they are in poverty. But money is only one of the resources. How many of the other resources a person has is very important to his/her happiness and economic stability. The more resources a person has in all areas, the easier it is to make changes and to live well. In short, the resources are interconnected. By that we mean having high levels of some or many of the resources makes it easier to build the rest.

The goal of this workbook is to help you become economically stable by improving all areas of your life. Building a solid balance of resources will free you from the "What It's Like Now" trap.

FINANCIAL	Having enough income to purchase goods and services and to save or invest money. Having an educated understanding of how money works – being fiscally literate.
EMOTIONAL	Being able to choose and control emotional responses, particularly to negative situations without engaging in self-destructive behavior. This is the "state of mind" that determines the way we think, feel, and behave at any given moment. This is an internal resource and shows itself through stamina, perseverance, and choice. This is about interpersonal skills like teamwork, teaching others, leadership, negotiation, and working with people from many backgrounds.
MENTAL	Having the mental ability and acquired skills (reading, writing, computing) to deal with daily life. This includes how much education and training a person has in order to compete in the workplace for good-paying jobs.
FORMAL REGISTER	Having the vocabulary, language ability, and negotiation skills to succeed in work and/or school environments.
SPIRITUAL	Believing in divine purpose and guidance and/or having a rich cultural connection that offers support and guidance.
INTEGRITY AND TRUST	Trust is linked to two issues: predictability and safety. Can I know with some certainty that this person will do what he/she says? Can I predict with some accuracy that it will occur every time? The second part of the question is safety: Will I be safe with this person?
PHYSICAL	Having physical health and mobility.
SUPPORT SYSTEMS	Having friends, family, and backup resources available to access in times of need. These are external resources.
RELATIONSHIPS/ ROLE MODELS	Having frequent access to adults who are appropriate, who are nurturing, and who don't engage in self-destructive behavior.
MOTIVATION AND PERSISTENCE	Having the energy and drive to prepare for, plan, and complete projects, jobs, and personal changes.
KNOWLEDGE OF HIDDEN RULES	Knowing the unspoken cues and habits of both middle class and wealth.

ADDITIONAL INFORMATION ON THE RESOURCES IN GENERAL

These resources cover every aspect of life, and every one of them is important. This workbook will only scratch the surface of what there is to know about each resource because our purpose is to examine our whole situation, not just one resource or another. At the end of the workbook we will make plans for the resources we want to build up. Right now, it's important to know that there are workbooks similar to this one for almost every resource. It would be good to start thinking now about which resources we might want to build up.

ADDITIONAL INFORMATION ON FINANCIAL RESOURCES

There are a number of workbooks and many books about what is called "fiscal literacy." Another way of saying this is: Everyone needs to know how to play the money game. In the money game there are no people in the bleachers and no cheerleaders; everyone is a player. The only question is: How well can you play? Most schools don't teach this important information, and yet it's crucial to the economic security of each of us. That leaves the teaching about money to our parents who may or may not be very good at the game themselves.

The facilitator will share a mental model on money that will give us a small taste of what we need to learn. At the end of the workbook is a list of resources, including information on fiscal literacy.

ADDITIONAL INFORMATION ON EMOTIONAL RESOURCES

Our emotional resources affect how successful we'll be with this workbook and in this class, so we want to explain some key concepts that can help us right away.

Poverty, addiction, abuse, and other dangerous situations can create in us reactions and patterns of behavior that work against us. They can create thoughts, feelings, and behaviors that are weak. For example, we might think, *I can't do this, I'm no good, It's all my fault,* or *It's all someone else's fault.* We might feel sorry for ourselves, useless, ashamed, angry, or self-destructive. We might blame others, whine, waste time, manipulate others, give up, hurt ourselves, or hurt others. If this is our way of looking at the world and ourselves, it will be hard to complete our plans and take the action steps necessary to get out of the trap of poverty.

In "Empowerment: A Course in Personal Empowerment" the writers say, "The single most important skill of the Empowerment Skills Training is the ability to *regulate* what you think and feel inside yourself – meaning that you decide the content, nature, and intensity of what you think, feel, and do.

"Regulating what you think and feel inside yourself does *not* mean, 'suppressing,' 'keeping the lid on,' 'putting up with it,' 'ignoring it,' or 'holding it in.'

"To regulate means to adjust the degree, intensity, and meaning of internal experience. It works like an internal thermostat that keeps the temperature inside where you want it, regardless of the temperature outside."

For one man, it was his older brother who taught him how to regulate his own emotions. He says, "For some reason, my older brother loved to beat me up. To get me mad he would push my buttons. And believe me, he knew them all. I would explode and start swinging; then he could 'defend' himself and happily twist me into knots. One day, in a rare moment of kindness [and candor], he said, 'Why do you let me do that to you? You know I love to piss you off so I can beat you up. Why do you fall for it every time?' At that moment I realized that the control for what happened was in me, not in him. I had always said, 'He makes me lose my temper. He made me do it.' From that day forward my thinking changed. I never gave that power to someone else again, including my brother. The power over my thinking and feeling is in me."

The facilitator will share exercises on how to regulate our emotions. When we can regulate our emotions, we will have a powerful way of living.

ADDITIONAL INFORMATION ON SUPPORT SYSTEMS

In *Bowling Alone* (2000), Robert Putnam describes social capital (or support systems) as something that is just as important as financial capital. He is talking about our connections with others, our networks, the things we do for each other with the trust and knowledge that they would do the same for us. Well-connected people feel a mutual obligation to help others; they have "favor banks." One man said, "It's like the golden rule. I'll do this for you now knowing that, down the road, you will return the favor."

Individuals have social capital, and so do communities. While individuals have a lot of connections with other individuals, communities have a lot of clubs and organizations like bowling leagues, service groups, unions, religious organizations, and so on.

There are two important types of social capital: *bonding* and *bridging*.

Bonding social capital is what we have with our tightest friends. It's exclusive, keeping others out. It's about belonging and identity. Others in our bonded group have many of the same resources and connections that we do. Some examples of bonding capital are ethnic fraternal organizations, church-based reading groups, and country clubs. Some bonding groups are harmful, such as gangs, the Ku Klux Klan, or people in certain neighborhoods that have the NIMBY (Not In My Back Yard) attitude.

Bridging social capital is what we have with people outside our usual circle; it is inclusive of people from different backgrounds. Examples of bridging capital are the civil rights movement, youth service clubs, chamber of commerce, United Way, and so on. When you have bridging capital, you may not have close friendships, but you do have many acquaintances and connections.

Putnam says bonding capital is good for getting by, while bridging capital is good for getting ahead. By this he means that our bonding-capital friends will have the same contacts and knowledge of job opportunities as we have. But someone outside our normal circle will have a number of contacts that we don't have and might be able to give us good leads for jobs or other resources.

> By the end of the twentieth century
> the gap between the rich and poor in the United States
> had been increasing for nearly three decades,
> the longest sustained increase in inequality in at least a century,
> coupled with the first sustained decline in social capital
> in at least that long.
>
> — Robert Putnam, *Bowling Alone*

ACTIVITY

We are going to create two mental models that will help us evaluate our own social capital.

'SOCIAL CAPITAL' MENTAL MODEL

1. Use a full sheet of paper to create a mental model. Draw a small circle inside a larger circle. The center of the circles represents you.

2. Thinking of the circles as a pie, draw eight pieces of pie and write the following labels around the outside of the larger circle: Household, Other Family, Friends, Work, School, Clubs and Organizations, Religious/Spiritual Group, and Formal Institutions/Agencies.

3. In each section of the pie, put the initials of the people who are in your life. Those with bonding relationships will be in the inner circle, while those with bridging capital will go in the outside circle.

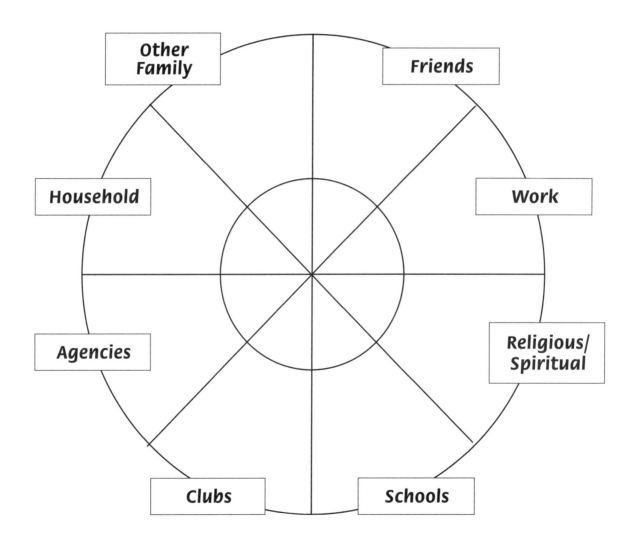

'SUPPORT FOR CHANGE' MENTAL MODEL

1. Use a full sheet of paper to create another mental model. Draw a small circle about 1 inch across in the middle of the page. This represents you.

2. Around the circle that represents you, place a number of circles representing important people in your life.

3. Label each of the circles that surround you by name – or use their initials.

4. Now imagine that you plan to make a big change in your life. Say, for example, you decide to go back to school, change jobs, or move to a new place to live. How will the people around you react to the change you want to make?

5. If they will give you total support and even help you make the change, draw a big thick line between that person and you.

6. If they would be totally against it, leave it blank.

7. If their support is halfhearted or weak, use a thin or dotted line.

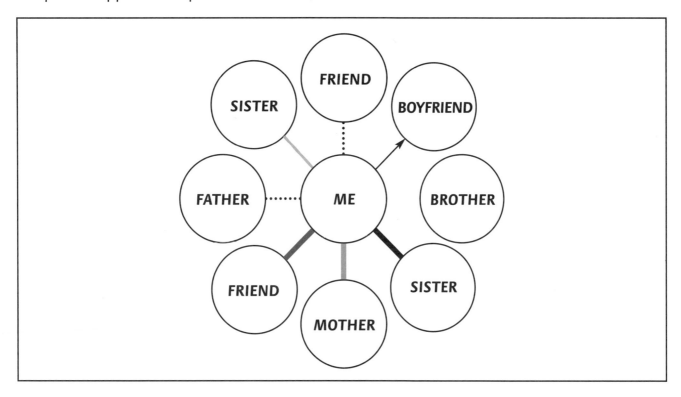

Now you have identified the people who will give you the most support and help when you need to change. There are some people who are neither helpful nor harmful, people who are neutral about changes that you may want to make. There are also some people who may be harmful to you in that they will actively oppose your efforts to change.

8. Identify the harmful people by circling their names or initials in some other color.

9. Finally, take the names of the people who are supportive and those who are harmful and put them on the "support for change" mental model. Mark them clearly, so that you can see who is going to be most helpful and who is going to be harmful.

DISCUSSION

1. This mental model is about just one change you might want to make. If you were to make a different change, would the support from the people around you be different?
2. What do you see in your relationships when you look at these two mental models?
3. Was there a time in your past when these mental models would have looked different?
4. If you decided to make a change in the future, how would this information help you?
5. Does looking at this pattern today have an impact on what you see in your future?
6. How can you strengthen your social support system?
7. Which economic group do you think has the most social capital? Does it work for them?

REFLECTIONS REFLECTIONS **REFLECTIONS** REFLECTIONS REFLECTIONS
*In the space below, write or draw your thoughts and ideas
about your own bonding and bridging capital.*

ADDITIONAL INFORMATION ON MOTIVATION AND PERSISTENCE

Here are some things we know about change:

Change is always going to happen. Some changes we have no control over. Some we do. Change is not always easy. It takes wisdom, courage, and motivation to change. Let's investigate motivation by reviewing the work of William Miller and Stephen Rollnick, who wrote *Motivational Interviewing* (2002), and Steve Andreas and Charles Faulkner, who edited *NLP: The New Technology of Achievement* (1993). [Note: NLP stands for neurolinguistic programming.]

WISDOM AND VALUES

 We need wisdom to know what we should and can change. To figure out what we should change we need to understand our values.

Values describe what life means to us, what is important to us. They influence our motivation. We move toward the things that we value and away from things we don't. For example, if a woman values money highly, she will make decisions and take action toward things that make money. She will be motivated to make money. If a woman dreams of and values a certain house in a certain neighborhood, she will make choices and take steps to get that house. She is motivated to get that particular house. If a woman values relationships highly, she will make choices and do things that maintain those relationships. She will be motivated to keep relationships.

Some people become disconnected from their values. When that happens, they lose their motivation and end up sitting in front of the TV for hours, flipping through the channels. It's as if they've lost their purpose for living.

MOTIVATION

 Another thing we must have to change is motivation. Miller and Rollnick describe motivation as being ready, willing, and able.

'WILLING'

When we first think about changing something we put the idea on a scale. On one side of the scale is what we have now, and on the other is what we could have – or what we want. For us to be willing to change, the scale has to be tipped toward the "what we want" side – or toward the future. The scale tips back and forth while we figure out if the change is going to be worth all the effort it will take. Sometimes the change we want might be in conflict with other things we value. For example, we have already learned that *to achieve* we must give up some relationships, at least for a time. So ... if we want to go back to school (because we value education), the scale may tip back and forth between going to school and our desire to be with our friends.

The key to being willing is the size of the gap between what we have now and what we might have – the difference between what is and what could be. The bigger the difference, the more willing we will be to change.

Putting this in the casual register, one guy said, "Life is a s--- sandwich, and every day is another bite." This guy may not like s--- sandwiches, but he seems willing to eat one every day. If he was to recall what a bowl of cherries tasted like, he might decide to make some changes so that he could eat more cherries and less s---. The gap between what he has now and what he might have could help him become willing to change.

'ABLE'

To be *able* to change, we must feel confident that we can do what it takes, that we know the steps, and that we can imagine ourselves moving ahead. We have to think positively and be determined. When we want to change (when we're willing) but can't see a way to do it, we often shift back into thinking that we are fated, then slip into living for the moment again and so lose our motivation.

'READY'

To be *ready*, we have to move beyond the "I'll do it tomorrow" and the "yes, but" phase. This requires that we overcome our fear of failure *and* our fear of success and push through toward what we want.

Andreas and Faulkner say that motivation is a simple mental strategy that we can learn to use ourselves. They point out that we are always motivated for something. In fact, sometimes we are *too* motivated. Some of us are too motivated for chocolate, sex, cigarettes, and God knows what else. In that case, we have to learn some anti-motivation strategies, which includes self-control and impulse control.

But what happens when we see that big difference between what we have now and what we could have? What happens when the things we value seem out of reach? What do we need to do to get motivated?

Andreas and Faulkner also say there are two basic thinking strategies about motivation. Those who "move toward" what they want and those who "move away from" what they don't want.

CHARACTERISTICS OF 'MOVING TOWARD' THINKERS

- Jump out of bed in the morning, ready to go!
- Plan ahead for things they want to do, such as meet friends, go fishing, etc.
- Pick friends who keep them going, who interest them.
- Take advantage of opportunities when they arise.

Pros of Being 'Moving Toward' Thinkers

- Goal-oriented.
- Get things done.
- Get the jobs because they match what most employers are looking for.

Cons of Being 'Moving Toward' Thinkers

- Don't think through the problems carefully enough.
- Rush into things, putting the "pedal to the metal."
- Have to learn things the hard way.

CHARACTERISTICS OF 'AWAY FROM' THINKERS

- Lie in bed until the threats of what will happen become too great.
- Wait to change things until it really gets uncomfortable.
- Pick friends who don't bother them.
- Wait to change jobs until they just can't stand their job another minute.

Pros of Being 'Away From' Thinkers

- Careful about getting into things.
- Remember the bad times to stay motivated.
- Good at identifying and fixing problems.

Cons of Being 'Away From' Thinkers

- Afraid to try things.
- Get too involved in problems.
- When the pain and pressure to change are off, so is the motivation.
- Motivation comes and goes with the threats.
- Less attention is given to where they'll end up when they're looking back at the problem instead of looking ahead.
- Much higher stress, risk of health problems.

It's best if we learn to use both motivational strategies with an emphasis on the "moving toward" strategy. We can do this by monitoring our motivational strategies and practicing new ways of thinking and acting.

COURAGE

The Serenity Prayer has something to say about motivation:

*God, grant me the serenity
to accept the things I cannot change,
the courage to change the things I can,
and the wisdom to know
the difference.*

This can apply as much to what we are doing about poverty as it does to recovery from addiction.

When we think about change and motivation, we have to consider what we will do with our own life, as well as what we will do about poverty in our community. What can we change about ourselves? What can we change about our communities? When we have answered these questions, we'll know what it will take in the way of courage to move toward prosperity. By the way, the prosperity we're talking about here isn't just financial, it's an overall sense of well-being, success, contentment, and (yes) happiness.

*You know you're motivated when
you are the one making the argument for change
and not someone else.*

DISCUSSION

1. How does poverty impact what a person values?
2. What are some things that cause people to lose their motivation?
3. How would you know when you are willing to change?
4. How much do you value moving out of poverty and toward economic stability?
5. What can help you feel confident about moving toward economic stability?
6. How would you know when you are ready for change?
7. Which motivational strategy do you tend to use the most?
8. What would it be like if you used the "moving toward" strategy more often?

In the space below, write or draw your thoughts
about motivation and change.

REFLECTIONS REFLECTIONS REFLECTIONS REFLECTIONS REFLECTIONS REFLECTIONS REFLECTIONS REFLECTIONS

ACTIVITY

Activity: Case studies ... It's important to become good at analyzing a person's resources because, before we're done, you'll need to do a self-assessment of your own resources. The best way is to analyze some case studies. It's good practice.

Time: 30-90 minutes

Materials: Case studies provided by facilitator

Procedure: 1) Do one case study at a time.

2) Read and score each case study by yourself.

3) Share your scores with others and discuss how you came to your decision. It is important that each person gets good at tight thinking. One of the best ways is to hear what others think, so you can sort out and explain your own ideas. It's OK to build on the ideas of others.

4) Look for the person's strong and weak resources. It's the strong resources that he/she will use to build the others.

Create your own case study: Think of someone you know who has achieved economic stability and interview him/her about his/her resources. Report back to the group what you learn.

DISCUSSION

When the group has analyzed several case studies – enough to be able to do tight thinking about the resources – discuss these questions.

1. Which resources does poverty impact the most severely?

2. Which resources are the hardest to assess?

3. Which resources do you think are the most important in order to have a well-balanced life?

4. As the group worked through the case studies, in what ways did the thinking about the resources get tighter?

USING THIS INFORMATION

Dale is a 34-year-old white man who was raised in poverty. He's still in poverty, but this story is about the beginning of his transition out. He's a high school dropout who has worked a series of jobs, the best one a manufacturing job in a mid-sized city in Ohio. He has moved frequently, living in a number of states with a number of different women. After a recent divorce, he returned to Ohio looking for work and is living with some friends. Dale wants custody of his daughter because his ex-wife has a serious mental health problem. The only way to get custody, though, is to establish a home. Dale's strongest resources are emotional, physical, and motivational. His weakest resources are financial, support systems, and knowledge of the hidden rules of middle class.

Dale applied at the manufacturing plant several times with no results before beginning *Getting Ahead*. He decided to try again, using what he had learned about economic class.

He went to the plant to apply, this time not just dropping off the application and walking away, but staying to talk to the secretary taking the forms. He explained why he wanted the job (establish economic security, get custody of his daughter) and told the office worker that he had worked there before and knew how to do the work. He then asked about a man who had worked at the plant when he first worked there years earlier. It turned out that the man was now in management. The secretary made a call and arranged for Dale to see the manager right then.

When Dale went into the office he was fidgeting and stumbling over his language when he thought, *I've got to just go for it.* Again he explained himself, how he wanted to provide for his daughter, get and keep a good job, establish a home, and how he was at the point in his life where he knew he had to make a major change. The manager was impressed and told Dale he could have the job, but there was one thing he would have to do first. He would have to cut off his ponytail. The plant was under new management and one of the rules that had changed was the one about ponytails. One man who had worked there for years quit his job rather than cut his hair. Dale recognized this as a conflict in hidden rules and chose to give up his ponytail for the job. The job pays a living wage and provides benefits. Dale moved to a small apartment near the plant so he could save money.

DISCUSSION

1. What resources was Dale trying to build?
2. What resources did he use? How did he use them?
3. What hidden rules did he use? How did he use them?
4. How did Dale use mediation when talking with the manager?
5. How much did it matter that the manager had no idea about the hidden rules as they're taught here?
6. Which motivational strategy did Dale use?
7. What will Dale need to do to maintain his changes?

Use the space below to write or draw your own thoughts
about resources and finding a balance in life.

REFLECTIONS REFLECTIONS REFLECTIONS REFLECTIONS REFLECTIONS

NEW NEW NEW NEW NEW **VOCABULARY** NEW NEW NEW NEW NEW

Words	Meanings

MODULE 7

Stages of Change

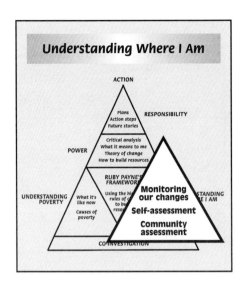

Understanding Where I Am

Learning Objectives

WHAT'S COVERED	WHY IT'S IMPORTANT	HOW IT'S CONNECTED TO YOU
You will: Develop a working definition of what it means to be motivated. Learn the "stages of change." Assess your stage of change. 	This information is important because we need to be in charge of our own changes. All too often others are doing assessments on us and giving us plans to complete. Part of taking charge of our life is making and monitoring our own changes. This information helps us think about where we are.	Earlier we covered the theory of change for this work. We said that people in poverty needed to move to the abstract to get new ideas. The "stages of change" was one of the three areas that needed to be explored. At the time we begin planning, we'll need to come back to this information. Until then, keep testing yourself and see where you are in the stages of change.

In his "stages of change" model, William Miller names five stages. We go through these stages just about every time we make a change. Being aware of the stages can help us move through them more effectively.

Stages of Change	
1. Pre-contemplation	We aren't even thinking about changing. We may not know how, so we don't concern ourselves with it. We may not have suffered much, so we don't see the need. We aren't willing.
Example: Take someone (let's say a woman) who has been smoking a long time. She knows it's bad for her health, but she's annoyed by everyone harping about it. The more others push for her to quit, the more it feels like her rights and freedoms are being challenged. She doesn't ever expect to change and, what's more, doesn't want to.	

	Stages of Change
2. Contemplation	We're concerned and worried, and we begin considering a change, but we're not sold on it yet. This stage is all about thinking. We can be in this stage for a long time. Knowing this, we might be able to move through it more quickly. There are two important things that have to be dealt with in this stage: ambivalence and identity.
	Ambivalence: This is when we want to change but don't want to change. We think of the costs and benefits – what we'll gain and what we'll lose. We think about our peers, how we'll keep the respect of the people around us if we make a change. We worry about what people will think or say about us.
	Identity: We worry that we won't be the same person if we change. Will the people who are in our lives now reject us if we change? Fear of failure becomes a part of this, and so does fear of success. We wonder what will happen if we do or don't change. Most of all we think, *When it doubt, put it off!*

Example: Something happens that makes the woman in our story start thinking. Someone she knows dies of cancer; a child asks her to quit, or she gets disgusted with the way her clothes smell. She stays on the fence for a long time, thinking, "I'm a smoker. Always have been, always will." That identity is hard to change.

3. Prevention	For the first time, we begin to make the argument for change, not the others who always seem to know what's best for us. That is a sign that we're motivated. We think, "I'm going to change, and I'm figuring out what to do." We intend to change in the near future. We're in transition, so we make small behavior changes and play the "yes/but" game.

Example: Our smoker has decided to stop smoking – but only kind of. She switches to low-tar/nicotine cigarettes, tries to smoke less, might try patches, or even quits for a few days, but she doesn't tell her friends what she's trying to do.

4. Action	We're doing it, but it's shaky. We make a public commitment to the change, we've made a plan, and we're trying to stick to it. When we have some success we begin to think we can do it. Identity may not have changed yet, but we're thinking differently.

Example: Our smoker still thinks of herself as a smoker, and she promises never to be like others who quit and become crusading anti-smokers. Her plan develops out of the preparation phase, and she now takes a behavioral class and uses patches. She even has a plan to prevent relapse, and she tries to keep the back door of her commitment closed so she won't run out that back door the first time she runs into trouble.

5. Maintenance	I've done it, now I'm working at keeping it. But it's not a sure thing. Many things can trigger a relapse, so plans have to be used for some time. Efforts have to be made to prevent relapse – and to recover from relapse quickly if/when it occurs.

Example: Our non-smoker works hard to stay smoke-free and begins to gain real confidence in herself as the time passes. Her identity slowly changes, and she's at ease with her new lifestyle.

ACTIVITY

Activity: Evaluating your own changes

Time: 10 minutes

Materials: Scratch paper or use the space below

Procedure: 1) Think of a change you made and write or draw out the story.

2) Identify with a colored marker, or a mark on your drawing, to show where the stages of change took place in your story.

3) Share your story with another person and listen to his/her story. Help each other identify how and when the stages took place.

DISCUSSION

Make a list as you discuss these questions:

1. What do most people say are reasons they can't change? What barriers to change are caused by individuals in poverty?

2. What barriers to change are created by living in the tyranny of the moment – by poverty itself?

3. What barriers to change are created by agencies?

4. What barriers to change are created by the community and political/economic structures?

5. What is the hardest thing about changing?

NEW NEW NEW NEW NEW **VOCABULARY** NEW NEW NEW NEW NEW

Words	Meanings

MODULE 8

Self-Assessment Regarding Resources

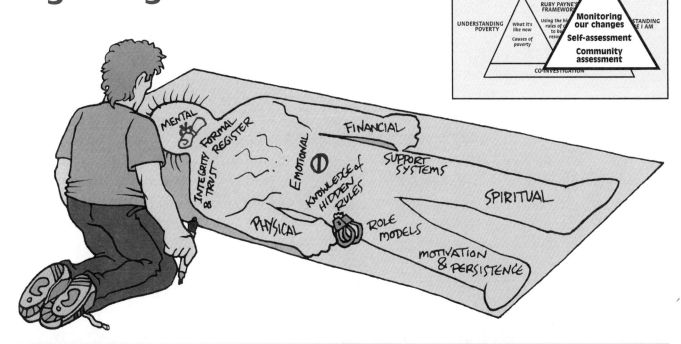

Understanding Where I Am

ACTION

Plans
Action steps
Future stories

RESPONSIBILITY

Critical analysis
What it means to me
Theory of change
How to build resources

POWER

RUBY PAYNE'S FRAMEWORK

UNDERSTANDING POVERTY

What it's like now

Using the hidden rules of g to bu reso

Monitoring our changes

Self-assessment

Community assessment

STANDING E I AM

Causes of poverty

CO-INVESTIGATION

Learning Objectives

WHAT'S COVERED

You will:

Do a self-assessment of your own resources.

Create a mental model summarizing your own resource levels.

Create a list of strategies for building each resource.

Create a list of hidden rules that would be needed to build each resource.

WHY IT'S IMPORTANT

The 11 resources cover all aspects of life. It's important to do your own assessment of your whole life, not just pieces of the "What It's Like Now" mental model.

HOW IT'S CONNECTED TO YOU

We have covered the information we need in order to have an accurate picture of our economic situation.

We've investigated political/economic systems and learned about hidden rules, language issues, and resources.

Now it's time to use this information to make changes.

The first step is to do an accurate assessment of our own resources. When we're done with this, we'll do an assessment of the community, then start making our own plans.

ACTIVITY

Activity: Self-assessment
Time: 45-60 minutes
Materials: Worksheets
Procedure: 1) Before you begin doing this activity, stop and think: How are you going to approach this? What attitude are you going to take? This investigation takes two things: tight thinking and honesty. It's important that you make a commitment to giving this your best shot. Choose your attitude as if your future depends on it, because in a real sense it does.

2) Review all the mental models you have created for yourself as you worked your way through this workbook: "What It's Like Now," "Social Capital," and "Support for Change." Make any necessary changes in order to keep them accurate and up-to-date.

3) Are you willing to share your thinking and scores with others? Sometimes listening to others can help clarify one's thinking. At the same time, remember that this assessment is yours, not what someone else is saying about you.

4) Complete the following checklist on your own, each person working individually. If a question doesn't make sense, ask the co-facilitator to explain it.

5) There are 11 sets of questions, one for each resource. On the right, beside the "yes" and "no" columns, is a column with the words Low Resources, Medium Resources, and High Resources (if you mark a "yes" in the row).

6) These worksheets are not a scientific scoring scale, but they *can* help you do accurate thinking about your resources. After you have worked through each resource, you will be asked to circle the final score you give yourself. Look at where you marked the most yeses and think about the meaning of the questions.

7) One final thought before you begin: Do these worksheets as if they were just another case study. Look at the impact that poverty has had on you from the outside. Try to separate yourself from the problems in order to see them more clearly.

8) Sometimes doing a self-assessment can be painful, especially if a number of our resources are very low. It would be natural to want to cut ourselves some slack, to take it easy on ourselves, but this is the time to do tough, tight thinking. At the same time we can celebrate our strongest resources. It is those resources that will help us build other resources.

Financial Resources			
Self-Assessment Questions	Y	N	
Do you have the skills to live in the survival mode for the next few years? Do you go to payday or cash-advance lenders? Do you live in a shelter, transitional housing, or subsidized housing? Do you buy furniture, appliances, or entertainment equipment from lease/purchase, or rent/own outlets? Do you use government assistance programs – food stamps, TANF (Temporary Assistance for Needy Families), a medical card? Do you make less than a living wage? Do you work a full 40-hour week? Do you have a debt-repayment plan that you follow?			**Low Resources**
Do you have a written budget that you follow? Do you receive medical benefits, vacation, and sick leave from work? Do you pay less than 35% of your income for housing? Do you use regular banking services like checking and savings accounts? Do you make enough money to be able to save for emergencies? Do you own your own home? Do you make a living wage? Do you have investments in mutual funds, bonds, stocks, real estate? Do you have a pension plan? Do you own property or a business?			***Medium Resources***
Did you receive formal education on fiscal matters? Do you pay off credit-card debt each month? Keep a zero balance? Do you own intellectual property? Do you have a financial adviser or a firm that manages your finances?			***High Resources***

RANKING: Circle below the score you give yourself for financial resources.
1 =*very low resources,* 5 = *yes, I have all medium and high financial resources that give me financial stability.*

1	2	3	4	5

Emotional Resources		
Self-Assessment Questions	Y	N
Do you lose your temper and yell at others? Do you hit and fight others? Do you have substance abuse and mental health problems that affect housing, employment, and social interactions? Do you manipulate others to get what you want and need? Do you act before thinking? Do you blame others when things go wrong? Do you try to control the thoughts, feelings, and actions of others? Do you have to be threatened to get things done? Do you have rigid rules for how you and others should behave? Do you identify your feelings quickly and easily?		*Low Resources*
Do you usually solve problems with others by talking it through? Do you consider the thoughts and feelings of others? Do you usually know what you are feeling, then choose positive actions? Do you generally identify most of your choices before acting? Do you act on your own without having to have other people around? Do you use self-talk to help you deal with problems and stick to your plans?		*Medium Resources*
Do you set aside problems that are troubling you for a while so you can get your work done? Do you accept responsibility for your actions and not blame others? Do you get along well with people from other backgrounds and economic classes? Do you look for ways to grow in everything? Do you help others grow – and empower others and yourself?		*High Resources*

RANKING: Circle below the score you give yourself for emotional resources.
1 = *very low resources, 5 = yes, I can usually handle the toughest situations in positive ways.*

1	2	3	4	5

Mental Resources

Self-Assessment Questions	Y	N	
Do you often find yourself getting trapped in negative thinking? Do you frequently think about your fears and desires? Do you generally solve problems by trial and error? Do you read and write well enough to work in the service sector? Do you or could you do math well enough to count change and operate a calculator? Did you drop out of school before 12th grade and not return or get a GED? Do you or could you type, enter information on a computer, and use a word processor?			*Low Resources*
Do you or could you write business letters? Do you or could you file alphabetically and numerically – and know how to keep track of supplies? Do you fix cars and make home repairs yourself? Do you have a high school diploma or GED? Do you have vocational training after high school? Do you recognize your thoughts as you have them and choose helpful thoughts and feelings? Do you change the way you do things when old ways don't work? Do you solve problems by using logical procedural steps? Do you have mechanical and equipment operating skills? Do you have a trade, such as carpentry, plumbing, electrical? Do you have a certification in a trade or field of study? Do you have artistic skills and/or the ability to sing or play an instrument?			*Medium Resources*
Do you make detailed plans and carry them out? Do you have a college degree? Do you have a master's degree or doctorate?			*High Resources*

RANKING: Circle below the score you give yourself for mental resources.

1 = *very low resources,* 5 = *yes, I can use my knowledge, thinking skills, and education to compete in the world of work and hold good jobs.*

1	2	3	4	5

Spiritual Resources			
Self-Assessment Questions	Y	N	
Do you believe in fate – that your choices don't make a difference? Do you believe in good luck and bad luck and therefore make few choices? Do you sometimes get material help (clothing, food, emergency assistance) from a church or religious institution? Do you believe in a higher power and a purpose that is larger than yourself?			*Low Resources*
Do you have a spiritual life outside of organized religion? Do you have a social relationship with one or more members of a church? Do you belong to a church, temple, synagogue, or mosque where you are active with others? Do you have an ethnic or racial culture that gives you guidance, help, and strength?			*Medium Resources*
Do you believe that choices you make today will affect your future? Do you attend religious activities and/or worship periodically? Do you have respect for others and understand your connections to others?			*High Resources*

RANKING: Circle below the score you give yourself for spiritual resources.
1 = *very low resources, 5 = yes, I have spiritual resources that help me move toward an honest, generous, and productive life.*

1	2	3	4	5

Physical Resources		
Self-Assessment Questions	Y	N
Do you need help to care for your own body? Do you get sick often? Do you use free clinics? Do you engage in risky behaviors that create health problems? Do you have any addictions or mental illnesses? Do you have any stress-related illnesses? Do you have any other chronic illness? Do you have problems with your teeth? Do you have weight problems? Do you care for someone whose illness or age requires a great deal of your time and energy? Do you have medical coverage, including Medicaid? Do you have Medicaid coverage for your children? Do you have public coverage for your children – but no Medicaid?		Low Resources
Do you have the health to work regularly? Do you have the ability to drive? Do you have the ability to do hard physical work? Do you have the ability to work in construction and repair? Do you have the ability to do fine craftsmanship? Do you generally eat healthy, balanced meals?		Medium Resources
Do you have medical coverage through an employer? Do you have medical and prescription coverage through an employer? Do you get regular exercise? Do you have physical beauty? Do people often comment that you are attractive? Do you have at least average athletic ability in more than one sport? Do you have excellent health?		High Resources

RANKING: Circle below the score you give yourself for physical resources.
1 = *very low resources*, 5 = *yes, I feel that I have the physical resources to work in any setting with any group of people.*

1	2	3	4	5

Social Support Resources			
Self-Assessment Questions	Y	N	
Do you have fewer than two supportive people in your life? For support, do you have only case managers and other professionals? Do you live in an unsafe neighborhood? Do people in your immediate circle hold you back from making changes? Do you distrust many of the people who live around you? Are family and friends rarely available to you? Are your family members rigid (pretty much just one way) in the way they try to deal with problems? Does your "bonding capital" include people who are harmful or dangerous to you and/or children?			*Low Resources*
Are family and friends usually available to help you in times of need? Does your bonding capital include people who are positive and helpful to you and/or children? Do you belong to a club or group that meets regularly? For example, a bowling league, softball team, service club, church, recovery group, special-interest group? Do you have "bridging capital" where there are people from different areas and backgrounds, people with different resources and hidden rules?			*Medium Resources*
Are positive and supportive family and friends almost always available to you? Do you have a large network of professional colleagues? Do you have extensive political, social, and financial connections?			*High Resources*

RANKING: Circle below the score you give yourself for social support resources.
1 = *very low resources, 5 = yes, I have a social support system that is positive and helpful.*

1	2	3	4	5

Relationships and Role Model Resources			
Self-Assessment Questions	Y	N	
Do you have people at home and in your family who are negative or destructive to you, themselves, or others? Do you have friends in school or at work who are destructive or negative to you, themselves, or others? Are there people in your neighborhood who are destructive or negative to you, themselves, or others?			*Low Resources*
Do you have people in your life who will give steady support to you and whatever positive changes you make? Do you have many relationships of mutual respect with people at work or in your profession? Do you have someone you can model yourself after in one or more areas of your life?			*Medium Resources*
Do you have one or more mentors – people who coach or guide you in one or more areas of your life? Do you act as mentor for anyone else?			*High Resources*

RANKING: Circle below the score you give yourself for relationships and role model resources. 1 = *very low resources*, 5 = *yes, I have relationships and role models who are positive and helpful.*

1	2	3	4	5

Knowledge of Hidden Rules Resources			
Self-Assessment Questions	Y	N	
Do you have conflicts with your spouse or other family members over the hidden rules of class? Do you ever get into economic-class conflicts at work? Do you ever get into economic-class conflicts with people who work in agencies?			*Low Resources*
Have you given up any relationships for achievement at work or in school? Do you know and use the hidden rules to successfully hold an hourly wage job? Do you have strategies for solving conflicts positively?			*Medium Resources*
Do you know and use the hidden rules to successfully hold a mid-level management job? Do you know and use the hidden rules to successfully hold a top management job? Do you know and use the hidden rules to build resources and a well-balanced life?			*High Resources*

RANKING: Circle below the score you give yourself for knowledge of hidden rules.
1 = *very low resources*, 5 = *yes, I use my knowledge of hidden rules effectively.*

1	2	3	4	5

Language Formal Register Resources		
Self-Assessment Questions	Y	N
Do you use the casual register of language only? Do you feel uncomfortable around people who use the formal register? Do you use the circular story pattern almost all the time?			Low Resources
Are you able to speak in the formal/consultative register, with proper syntax and grammar? Do you write in the formal/consultative register? Do you use language to negotiate and solve problems? Do you have a large vocabulary? Do you use abstract terms to express complex ideas?			Medium Resources
Do you have the ability to be "bilingual"? In other words, do you translate formal register to the casual register when necessary? Do you use the formal register to develop and maintain your profession? Do you use the formal register to direct policy and/or the direction of an organization?			High Resources

RANKING: Circle below the score you give yourself for knowledge of formal register resources. 1 = *very low resources*, 5 = *yes, I can use the formal register of language skillfully.*

1	2	3	4	5

Integrity Resources			
Self-Assessment Questions	Y	N	
Do you often deceive others? Do you lie frequently? Do you obey the laws – but only when they're enforced? Do you make decisions in your own best interest only?			*Low Resources*
Are you a truthful person? Do you try to do what is fair and right for all concerned? Do you think it's wrong to break the law – even if you don't caught? Do you take responsibility for yourself but sometimes blame others?			*Medium Resources*
Do you take on difficult problems and accept responsibility for yourself – and not blame others? Do you take on tough issues, accept responsibility for yourself, and make yourself accountable to others? Do you try to do what will be beneficial to all concerned?			*High Resources*

RANKING: Circle below the score you give yourself for integrity.
1 = *very low resources, 5 = yes, I can be trusted to make legal, moral, and ethical decisions and take responsibility for my actions.*

1	2	3	4	5

Motivation and Persistence Resources			
Self-Assessment Questions	Y	N	
Do you often have low energy? Do you watch TV too much? Would you rather not be promoted at work? Do you dislike learning? Do you work hard but pretty often goof off while on the job? Do you give up easily? Do you work only for the money? Do you avoid promotions and training? Do you tend to wait until things get unbearable before you make changes?			**Low Resources**
Do you stick to the goals you set until you finish them? Do you set short-term goals? Do you plan for and make positive changes? Do you have fairly steady energy? Do you try to be right? Do you seek promotion for the power or recognition?			**Medium Resources**
Do you generally have high energy and try to do the right thing for the business or organization? Do you seek out training? Do you see opportunities coming and prepare yourself for them? Do you enjoy and seek out learning on your own? Do you pursue promotion because it reflects excellence?			**High Resources**

RANKING: Circle below the score you give yourself for motivation and persistence.
1 = *very low resources*, 5 = *yes, I have the motivation and persistence to move toward the things that I need and to make changes.*

1	2	3	4	5

RESOURCES MENTAL MODEL

In the table below, color in the amount of each resource to match what you did above. This is one more mental model to add to your personal guidebook.

	Financial	Emotional	Mental	Spiritual	Physical	Social	Relational	H. Rules	Language	Integrity	Motivation
5											
4											
3											
2											
1											

DISCUSSION

1. Looking at the mental model, which are your highest or strongest resources?

2. How might you use the high resources to build other resources?

3. How did you get the high resources that you have? Did someone teach you or show you the way? Was it something inside you, a decision you made, or a way of thinking? Was it a gift or talent?

4. What did you learn about your situation and your life by doing this exercise?

5. Which resources are your lowest?

6. Was this activity hard to do – or easy? If it was hard to do, what made it hard?

7. Thinking back over everything that we have investigated so far, how does this piece fit into it?

8. How important is it to do an accurate and honest self-assessment?

9. What is the difference between doing your own assessment of your life and your resources and having an assessment done by someone working at an agency?

10. Where are you with regard to the stages of change now?

In the space below, write or draw your thoughts and ideas about your resources.

REFLECTIONS REFLECTIONS REFLECTIONS REFLECTIONS REFLECTIONS

NEW NEW NEW NEW NEW **VOCABULARY** NEW NEW NEW NEW NEW

Words	Meanings
_____	_____
_____	_____
_____	_____
_____	_____
_____	_____
_____	_____
_____	_____
_____	_____

MODULE 9

Building Resources

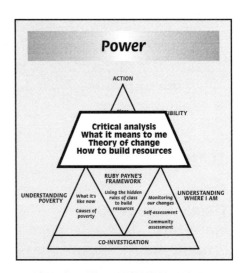

Power

ACTION

...IBILITY

**Critical analysis
What it means to me
Theory of change
How to build resources**

RUBY PAYNE'S FRAMEWORK

UNDERSTANDING POVERTY

What it's like now

Causes of poverty

Using the hidden rules of class to build resources

Monitoring our changes

Self-assessment

Community assessment

UNDERSTANDING WHERE I AM

CO-INVESTIGATION

Learning Objectives

WHAT'S COVERED	WHY IT'S IMPORTANT	HOW IT'S CONNECTED TO YOU
You will: Develop a list of ways to develop each resource. Develop a list of the hidden rules that would be needed to build each resource.	This is important because we can improve our lives by building our resources. The thinking we do in this module will help us make good plans. 	We keep adding to what we have learned before. We learned about resources, and we did a self-assessment. Now we're going to think through the details of how to build resources. We're going to go even deeper and think through which hidden rules we'll need to use to build each resource. When we put all these steps together, we'll be able to make our own plans for economic stability.

Building resources is easier said than done. If it were really easy, there would be very little poverty in the United States. It's now time to do our best thinking to find ways to help each other build resources. While you're doing this, keep three things in mind:

1. Building all our resources will give us a balanced life. Have you ever known of someone who had high financial resources but very low emotional and social support? Or have you known someone who was very smart but just couldn't get along with others? That person has high mental resources and low emotional resources; their resources are not balanced.

2. Beware of the tendency we all have to focus on building resources that are already high. Take for example, a woman who is beautiful and healthy. She has high physical resources already, so she probably doesn't need to focus on building that resource any more. But it wouldn't surprise anyone if she still focused on improving her health and beauty. This tendency is understandable. Working on resources where we're already strong isn't too hard; this is where we're pretty sure we'll be successful. So, when doing this activity, do your best to shift your focus to where it will do the most good.

3. We already know that poverty isn't just about the choices of the people in poverty. There are system issues that contribute to poverty too. Right now, though, we're focusing on our personal response to poverty. We need to be as tough on ourselves as we'll be tough on the system. We'll get back to system issues, but first, let's stay focused on how to build resources.

ACTIVITY

Activity: Building resources
Time: 30-45 minutes
Materials: Flip chart paper and markers
Procedure: 1) Choose one of the two strategies below to brainstorm ideas.
    2) Make sure that every one of the 11 resources is covered by the group.

Option 1: Tic-Tac-Toe Technique

1. Draw lines on a full page to make nine squares, three squares in a row, three rows. In other words, you would be making a tic-tac-toe design.

2. In each square draw three rows of circles, three circles in a row; each square would have nine circles in it.

3. In the center circle of the center square, write the main goal. It could be "prosperity," "high resources," "getting out of poverty," "economic stability," or whatever you want.

4. Put the resources your group wants to develop and write them into eight remaining circles in the center square.

5. Now take each of the eight ideas and write them again – but this time in the center circle of the square that matches the design in the center square.

6. Try to think of eight new ideas involving the central theme of the eight new boxes.

7. Continue the process until you've completed as much of the diagram as you can.

8. Make a list of the hidden rules that you would need to use to build each resource.

9. Evaluate your ideas.

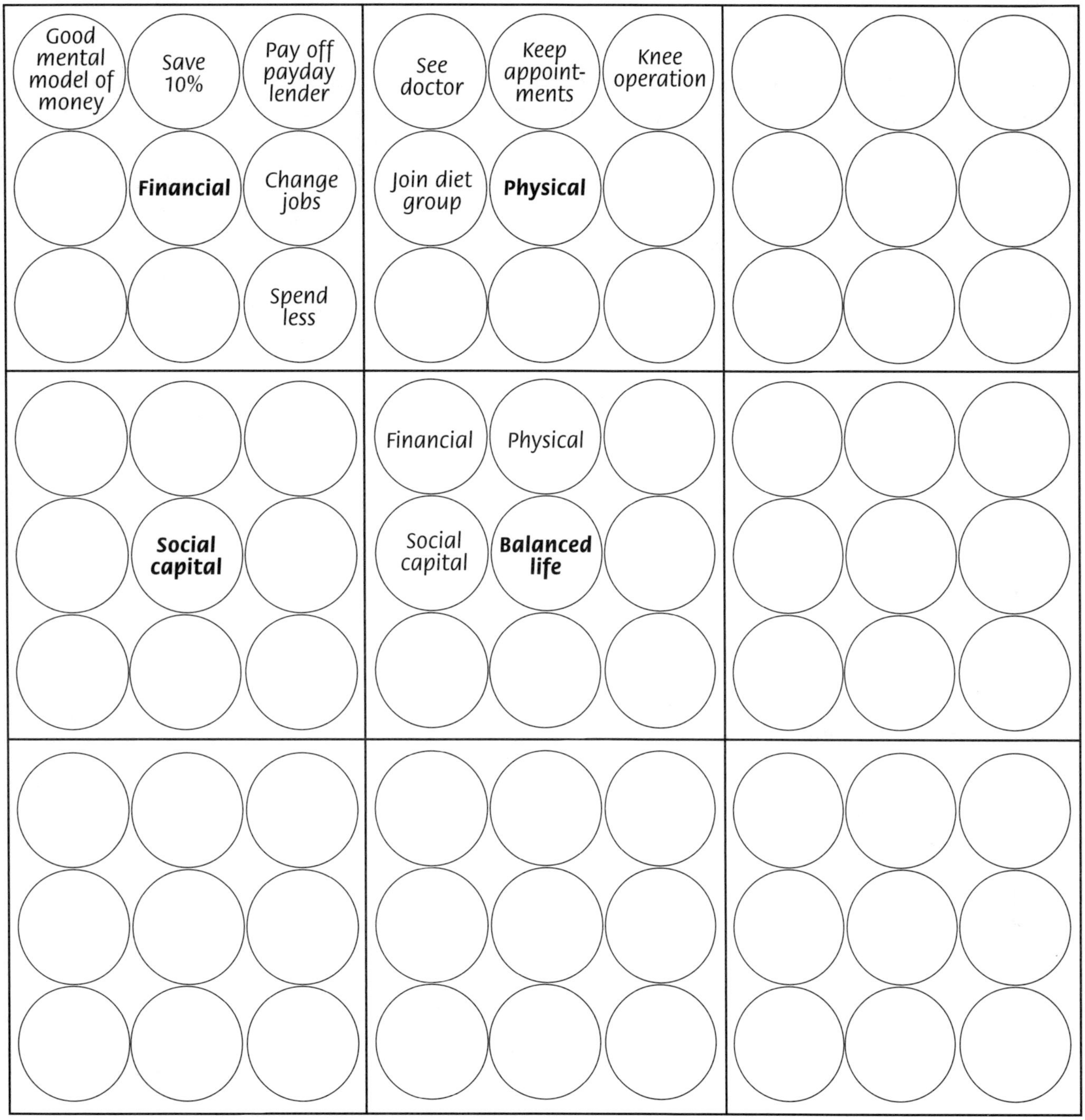

Panel 1 (top-left):
- Good mental model of money | Save 10% | Pay off payday lender
- (empty) | **Financial** | Change jobs
- (empty) | (empty) | Spend less

Panel 2 (top-center):
- See doctor | Keep appointments | Knee operation
- Join diet group | **Physical** | (empty)
- (empty) | (empty) | (empty)

Panel 3 (top-right): (all empty)

Panel 4 (middle-left):
- (empty) | (empty) | (empty)
- (empty) | **Social capital** | (empty)
- (empty) | (empty) | (empty)

Panel 5 (middle-center):
- Financial | Physical | (empty)
- Social capital | **Balanced life** | (empty)
- (empty) | (empty) | (empty)

Panel 6 (middle-right): (all empty)

Panel 7 (bottom-left): (all empty)

Panel 8 (bottom-center): (all empty)

Panel 9 (bottom-right): (all empty)

Option 2: Brainstorming

1. Working in groups at tables, with each table taking one or two resources, brainstorm ideas on how to build resources. When brainstorming, remember that you don't stop to criticize ideas; you want to let them flow so that different ideas spark new thinking. Using a flip chart, draw a line down the middle of the page from top to bottom. Then label the left side, "Building _____ Resources." List the ideas under that heading. Use one page for each resource.

Building _____ Resources	Hidden Rules

2. Label the right column "Hidden Rules." Now, under that heading, list the hidden rules that are needed to build that resource. Indicate which class's hidden rules would be needed – poverty, middle, or wealth. It's possible that one, two, or all three might be needed. For example, if you are working on building social support and decide that volunteering at a service agency will increase your bridging capital, what hidden rules would you need to use? Using the formal register would make things easier for the people you meet, so that's one option. You might think that it would be OK to use the casual register too, so in that case you would be using rules from two classes. It might also help if you used the middle-class rules for driving force (work and achievement) because, even though it's volunteer work you'll be doing, it will still be about achieving the goals of the organization. That is what you will need to be prepared to talk about. The middle-class rule on time is another that you might want to use. Nothing makes middle-class people happier than being able to rely on someone to be on time, every time.

3. Share ideas from all the tables and expand the brainstorming by letting the whole group suggest ideas.

4. Have a volunteer type up the list for all the resources so that everyone has a copy to look at when it's time to make individual plans.

DISCUSSION

1. What did you learn from this investigation?
2. How important is it that you change some of your resources?
3. Which resources were the most difficult to build? Why?
4. Did you get enough ideas for the resources you want to build to get you started?
5. Which resources were the easiest to build? Why?
6. When you listed the hidden rules that would be needed to build resources, what did you learn?
7. Which hidden rule of poverty was listed most often?
8. Which hidden rule of middle class was listed most often?
9. Which hidden rule of wealth was listed most often?
10. How did the group perform as problem solvers?
11. Where are you with regard to the stages of change now?

In the space below, write or draw your thoughts and ideas
about building your own resources.

REFLECTIONS REFLECTIONS REFLECTIONS REFLECTIONS REFLECTIONS

NEW NEW NEW NEW NEW **VOCABULARY** NEW NEW NEW NEW NEW

Words	Meanings

MODULE 10

Community Assessment

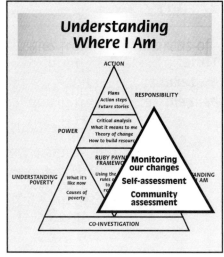

Understanding Where I Am

ACTION

RESPONSIBILITY

Plans
Action steps
Future stories

POWER

Critical analysis
What it means to me
Theory of change
How to build resources

RUBY PAYNE
FRAMEWO...

Monitoring our changes

UNDERSTANDING POVERTY

What it's like now

Using the rules o...
to...
re...

Self-assessment

...ANDING
...AM

Causes of poverty

Community assessment

CO-INVESTIGATION

Learning Objectives

WHAT'S COVERED
You will:

Complete an assessment of community resources.

Create a mental model to summarize community resources.

WHY IT'S IMPORTANT
It's important to do an assessment of the community because poverty is about more than the choices of the poor.

It's important to hold the community accountable for opportunities and protection of all its members and to create prosperity.

It's important that members of this group participate in solving community problems, not just their own.

HOW IT'S CONNECTED TO YOU
This goes back to the research continuum that was studied in MODULE 4. Our communities must have strategies from all four areas of research for fighting poverty. When we make our final plans about poverty, we'll need to include what we think needs to be done in the community.

ACTIVITY

Activity: Community assessment
Time: 30–45 minutes
Materials: Flip charts
Procedure:
1) As a group, complete the following tables.
2) Ask questions, investigate, and find out just what resources are available.
3) If necessary, have someone who knows about the topic come in and share with the group.
4) Remember, you are looking for strengths here, just as you were looking for strengths when you did the self-assessment of your own resources.

The questions are designed to help you get started; the group may want to add questions or information to make the study more complete. The "yes/no" columns are to register your general perception and the "?" column is to be checked if you need more information.

Community Resource: Housing and Banking			
Assessment Questions	Y	N	?
Does your community have programs to get people into home ownership quickly as a means for getting out of poverty? Is it effective? Does it reach a lot of people?			
Is rental property affordable?			
Does the shortage of affordable housing force people into living together in crowded conditions?			
Is the number of homeless people growing?			
Is "third sector" housing ownership (such as community land trusts, housing cooperatives, and mutual housing) present in your community?			
Does your community provide low-interest loans or microeconomic opportunities?			
Do the banks have high Community Reinvestment Act scores and/or high-quality strategic plans? Did community groups participate in developing the strategic plans?			

Does your community have sufficient and effective housing and banking strategies?

RANKING: Circle below the score you give the community for housing. 1 = *inadequate*, 5 = *yes, community housing programs and opportunities are sufficient and affordable.*

1	2	3	4	5

Community Resource: Wages			
Assessment Questions	Y	N	?
Does your community have a living-wage ordinance?			
Does your community attract and offer tax abatements to businesses that offer only low wages?			
Does your community have reasonable CEO-to-front-line-staff salary ratios in the private sector? In the public sector?			
Does your community have an unusually large number of employers who use temporary and part-time help as a means of avoiding the cost of healthcare benefits?			

Is your community committed to providing high wages for its people?

RANKING: Circle below the score you give the community for wages.
1 = *inadequate, 5 = yes, wages are good.*

1	2	3	4	5

Community Resource: Protection from Predators			
Assessment Questions	Y	N	?
Does your community permit payday lenders?			
If so, have any efforts been made to stop unfair practices?			
Does your community have sufficient and effective lending services for low-income families that could be used to replace lease/purchase stores?			
Does your community have an effective strategy for dealing with the illegal drug trade?			
Does your community have lending services that could be used to replace used-car dealers who prey on the poor?			
Does your community have an effective strategy for dealing with landlords who prey on the poor?			

Are low-income people in your community protected from predators?

RANKING: Circle below the score you give the community for predators. 1 = *inadequate, 5 = yes, the community is protected from predators, and low-income banking services are good.*

1	2	3	4	5

Community Resource: Job Opportunities			
Assessment Questions	Y	N	?
Are manufacturing jobs available?			
Are union jobs available?			
If so, is the starting pay a living wage, or has the union been forced to greatly lower its standards?			
Is training available for people in the service sector who want to move to the knowledge sector?			
Is training available for people in the manufacturing sector who want to move to the knowledge sector?			
Is anything being done about the "digital divide" – computer access and computer skills for low-income areas of the community and low-income families?			
Are good-paying jobs going out of the area in unusually high numbers?			
Is employee ownership widely available? Employee stock-ownership plans, profit-sharing plans, widely granted stock options?			
Is affordable, high-quality childcare available during working hours?			
Do employers consistently offer healthcare benefits?			

Does your community have sufficient jobs that pay well?

RANKING: Circle below the score you give the community for jobs.
1 = *inadequate*, 5 = *a plentiful supply of good-paying jobs is available.*

1	2	3	4	5

Community Resource: Education			
Assessment Questions	Y	N	?
Does school spending for poor children equal spending for middle-class and wealthy children?			
Do educators know how to help children from poverty learn quickly?			
Is the graduation rate improving?			
Is the dropout rate dropping?			
Are students prepared for the type of versatile workforce that is needed today?			
Do educators teach the rules of money management and investments to students?			
Are high-quality preschool opportunities available?			
Is Early Head Start available?			

Does your community have an educational system capable of helping poor children compete successfully in the workplace?

RANKING: Circle below the score you give the community for leadership. 1 = *inadequate*, 5 = *educators are on top of the issues and have successful programs in place.*

1	2	3	4	5

Community Resource: Transportation			
Assessment Questions	Y	N	?
Does the community have public transportation capable of moving poor people from their homes to the workplace, healthcare facilities, and agencies?			
Is public transportation affordable?			
Is public transportation safe?			
Is public transportation available at the hours needed to move people to and from work?			

Does your community have efficient and affordable transportation to move people to and from work?

RANKING: Circle below the score you give the community for transportation. 1 = *inadequate*, 5 = *public transportation is good.*

1	2	3	4	5

Community Resource: Health and Nutrition			
Assessment Questions	Y	N	?
Is healthcare affordable for people in poverty?			
Is healthcare available to people in poverty?			
Is healthcare accessible by public transportation?			
Is high-quality food available at local markets?			
Are poor neighborhoods environmentally safe?			
Are poor areas generally safe?			
Are mental health and addiction services available and affordable?			

Does your community have adequate preventive healthcare, healthcare, and good food available to people who are in poverty?

RANKING: Circle below the score you give the community for health issues. 1 = *inadequate*, 5 = *the community has a good system of healthcare for people in poverty.*

1	2	3	4	5

Community Resource: Leadership			
Assessment Questions	Y	N	?
Do city and/or regional planning leaders have strategies that assist people in poverty to move toward prosperity?			
Do development leaders have strategies that assist people in poverty to move toward prosperity?			
Do government leaders have strategies that assist people in poverty to move toward prosperity?			
Do social service sector leaders have strategies that assist people in poverty to move toward prosperity?			
Do business leaders have strategies that assist people in poverty to move toward prosperity?			
Do faith-based leaders have strategies that assist people in poverty to move toward prosperity?			
Do education leaders have strategies that assist people in poverty to move toward prosperity?			

Are your community leaders motivated and capable of moving the entire community toward prosperity?

RANKING: Circle below the score you give the community for leadership. 1 = *inadequate*, 5 = *community leaders are already doing what it takes to eliminate poverty.*

1	2	3	4	5

Now that you have done an assessment of community resources, put all your thinking into a mental model that summarizes the resources of the community. In the table below, color in the amount of each community resource copied from the tables on the previous pages.

COMMUNITY ASSESSMENT SUMMARY – MENTAL MODEL

Housing and Banking	Wages	Predators	Jobs	Education	Transportation	Health and Nutrition	Leadership
5	5	5	5	5	5	5	5
4	4	4	4	4	4	4	4
3	3	3	3	3	3	3	3
2	2	2	2	2	2	2	2
1	1	1	1	1	1	1	1

DISCUSSION

1. What are the strengths of your community?
2. What are the weaknesses of your community?
3. What problems do communities face when it comes to economic issues?
4. What opportunities does your community have in the near future?
5. List the local leaders who are committed to a wide range of strategies to eliminate poverty.
6. Does the group need to collect more information to have an accurate understanding of community resources?
7. Which agencies are most likely to fight for system changes to help people who are toward the bottom of the economic ladder?

REFLECTIONS REFLECTIONS **REFLECTIONS** REFLECTIONS REFLECTIONS
In the space below, write or draw your thoughts and ideas about
your community and the impact it has on your personal goals for getting out of poverty.

REFLECTIONS REFLECTIONS **REFLECTIONS** REFLECTIONS REFLECTIONS

NEW NEW NEW NEW NEW **VOCABULARY** NEW NEW NEW NEW NEW

Words	Meanings

MODULE 11

Your Plan
for Getting from
Poverty to Prosperity

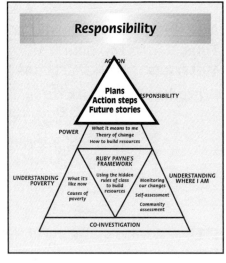

Learning Objectives

WHAT'S COVERED

You will:

Review mental models, notes, and stages of change.

List your strongest and weakest resources.

Rank the resources you need to work on.

Build plans for the first two or three resources.

Test your plans against SMART (Specific, Measurable, Attainable, Realistic, and Time-specific) goals.

Create immediate action steps.

WHY IT'S IMPORTANT

It's important that you make your own plans – plans that fit your whole situation and are based on your priorities.

HOW IT'S CONNECTED TO YOU

Everything we've done has been aimed at this and the next module. First, for you to have a plan that works for you. Then, for you to be a part of solving community problems.

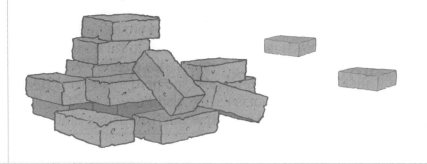

ACTIVITY

Activity: Creating your path out of poverty
Time: Two hours
Materials: Worksheets and mental models
Procedure: 1) Work through the following 10 steps very thoroughly.

2) Talk things over with other group members and the facilitator as you see fit.

3) If you are comfortable with sharing your work, share it with others so they can use your ideas to build their own plans.

STEP 1: Review all the mental models and notes that you've made in your workbook. They are:

- What It's Like Now

- Support for Change

- Social Capital

- Resources Self-Assessment

- Tic-Tac-Toe and/or Brainstorming Worksheet

- Community Assessment

STEP 2: List your three strongest resources and three weakest resources.

THREE STRONGEST RESOURCES

_____

_____

_____

THREE WEAKEST RESOURCES

_____

_____

_____

STEP 3: Rank the three resources that you choose to work on – the most important one first. These do not have to be the resources that are the lowest or weakest.

RANK THREE TOP RESOURCES TO WORK ON.	HOW IMPORTANT IS IT TO YOU THAT YOU CHANGE? 1-10 Scale: 1 = not important at all, 10 = very important	EXPLAIN IN YOUR OWN WORDS WHY CHANGE IS IMPORTANT TO YOU.
1.	Circle your score: 1 2 3 4 5 6 7 8 9 10	
2.	Circle your score: 1 2 3 4 5 6 7 8 9 10	
3.	Circle your score: 1 2 3 4 5 6 7 8 9 10	

STEP 4: Establish SMART goals for each of the three resources on your list. Before listing your goals, refer back to the work the group did about how to build resources. You also will find some ideas on the Tic-Tac-Toe mental model. It is *very important* that you set goals well. SMART goals are: Specific, Measurable, Attainable, Realistic, and Time-specific. Use a work-sheet to work on these goals first. When you have them exactly the way you want them, write them in the space on the following page.

Resource: Social Support
GOAL: One year from now, I will have more bridging social capital. I'll join two groups or organizations where I will have regular (at least monthly) contact with positive and diverse people.
Monitor for SMART standards: Check each box that meets the standards of a SMART goal. Get feedback from at least one other person that it is a SMART goal.
❏ Specific   ❏ Measurable   ❏ Attainable   ❏ Realistic   ❏ Time-specific

Example ...
Let's check to see if this example meets the SMART standard: *Is it specific?* Yes, it's about building bridging capital. *Is it measurable?* Yes, this person will join two groups and will have monthly contact. *Is it attainable or doable?* The answer to this is not so obvious. We would have to know more about the person making the goal, but let's say that most people could find the time to join two groups if it was important to them. *Is it realistic?* The answer to this is similar to the "attainable" question. *Is it time-specific?* Yes, it must be done within a year.

Resource:

GOAL:

Monitor for SMART standards: Check each box that meets the standards of a SMART goal. Get feedback from at least one other person that it is a SMART goal.

❏ Specific ❏ Measurable ❏ Attainable ❏ Realistic ❏ Time-specific

Resource:

GOAL:

Monitor for SMART standards: Check each box that meets the standards of a SMART goal. Get feedback from at least one other person that it is a SMART goal.

❏ Specific ❏ Measurable ❏ Attainable ❏ Realistic ❏ Time-specific

Resource:

GOAL:

Monitor for SMART standards: Check each box that meets the standards of a SMART goal. Get feedback from at least one other person that it is a SMART goal.

❏ Specific ❏ Measurable ❏ Attainable ❏ Realistic ❏ Time-specific

STEP 5: *Create procedural steps for each goal. Write the goal in the top space, put the procedural steps in a logical order, first things first. Identify the hidden rules that you think you will need to use. Finally, think out how long it will take to do each step and pick the starting date for each.*

Example ...

GOAL: One year from now I will have more bridging social capital. I'll join two groups or organizations where I will have regular (at least monthly) contact with positive and diverse people.		
STEPS:	**Hidden Rules**	**Starting Date**
1. Make a list of things that interest you and/or a list community issues that you want to do something about.	<u>Driving Force</u>: middle class = work and achievement.	Today
2. Find organizations that deal with those issues and interests.	<u>Language</u>: casual and formal registers, language to negotiate.	Today
3. Make contact – face to face or by phone, mail, or e-mail – with five organizations.	<u>Time</u>: middle class = keep the future in mind; be on time, reliable.	Tomorrow
4. Attend meetings and meet people from five organizations.	<u>Personality</u>: poverty = entertainment and humor; middle class = stability and achievement.	Two weeks from today
5. Sign up or join two of them.		Eight weeks from today for one, 12 weeks for the other
6. Attend meetings and get involved in a regular way.		

GOAL:		
STEPS:	**Hidden Rules**	**Starting Date**
1.		
2.		
3.		
4.		
5.		

GOAL:		
STEPS: 1. 2. 3. 4. 5.	**Hidden Rules**	**Starting Date**

GOAL:		
STEPS: 1. 2. 3. 4. 5.	**Hidden Rules**	**Starting Date**

STEP 6: *Make a list of where you will get help. When we begin to make changes, we almost always need the help of other individuals, groups, organizations, and agencies. Make a list for each goal.*

Example ...

GOAL:	Where to Get Help
1. Social Support	1. For ideas on interests: friends, family, people who are well-connected, newspapers, library, Internet. 2. For ideas on organizations and groups: newspaper, library, Internet, agency lists, chamber of commerce lists and phone book. Also talk to people outside of my bonding circle. 3. For first meeting: Find someone who is already connected or a member of the group and go with him/her. 4. If I don't know anyone, I can ask to meet with one person to find out what to expect. NOTE: Review the ideas this group created on how to build social support.

GOAL:	Where to Get Help
1.	
2.	
3.	

STEP 7: Weekly plan. Put the action steps you need to take into a weekly plan.

Example ...

GOAL 1:						
Sun	*Mon*	*Tue*	*Wed*	*Thu*	*Fri*	*Sat*
Read the paper; talk to family and friends; check phone book.	Chamber of commerce; agency lists; library; make lists of interests and organizations.	Make contact with two people.	Make contact with three people.	Research interests and organizations to see what's expected.	Talk with positive friends – people who support my changes.	Talk with positive friends – people who support my changes. Prepare plans for next week.

GOAL 1:						
Sun	*Mon*	*Tue*	*Wed*	*Thu*	*Fri*	*Sat*

GOAL 2:						
Sun	*Mon*	*Tue*	*Wed*	*Thu*	*Fri*	*Sat*

GOAL 3:						
Sun	*Mon*	*Tue*	*Wed*	*Thu*	*Fri*	*Sat*

STEP 8: Daily plan. On a 3-by-5 card, write down everything you're going to do today. Carry it with you and cross off the items as you get them done.

STEP 9: Create backup plans for when things go wrong. It's very easy to slip back into old ways of being. Sometimes we make wonderful plans for change but keep a back door open to escape if the going gets tough. We have to close the back doors so that we stick with our plans.

Example ...

Back Doors	How to Close Them
1. If things don't go well, I can always quit. (It's always easier to give up than keep trying.)	1. Recognize that you are about to fly out the back door. 2. Tell yourself that you can do this. Wait a few minutes, and the negative feeling will pass. 3. Talk to someone who supports what you're doing. Have his/her phone number handy and tell him/her ahead of time that it's his/her job to encourage you when things get rough. Have a sense of humor about this "order," but still be firm.
2. I'll do it tomorrow. Too much is going on today. I'll let it slide.	1. Recognize the negative thinking you are doing. 2. Make the phone call to your friend. 3. Tell yourself that nothing short of death or the house burning down is going to keep you from doing the one or two things on your daily list.
3. If the people around me don't get on board with this thing, I won't be able to do it.	1. Recognize the back-door thinking. 2. Make a list of people who do support your changes and stay in touch with them. 3. Have more than one plan for getting things done. If Person A won't help, have Person B ready to go. If Plan A falls apart, be ready with Plan B.

Back Doors	How to Close Them

STEP 10: *Share your plan with people whose support you're pretty sure of. This can include people in this group, the facilitator, friends, and family. The more support you can get, the more successful you'll be.*

DISCUSSION

1. How does it feel to have made your own plans for getting out of poverty?
2. Do you think of poverty differently now that you've completed your plans?
3. Before you began *Getting Ahead,* what was your future story? What did you tell yourself about the rest of your life? What did others tell you?
4. What is your future story now? What has changed?
5. What has this experience taught you about yourself?
6. Who else will benefit from your plans to get out of poverty?
7. Where are you with regard to the stages of change now?

In the space below, write or draw your thoughts, ideas, and feelings
about your personal path out of poverty.

REFLECTIONS REFLECTIONS REFLECTIONS REFLECTIONS REFLECTIONS REFLECTIONS

NEW NEW NEW NEW NEW **VOCABULARY** NEW NEW NEW NEW NEW

Words

Meanings

MODULE 12

Creating Mental Models for Your Personal Path Out of Poverty *and* for Community Prosperity

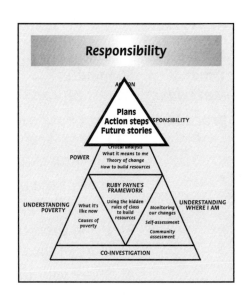

Learning Objectives

WHAT'S COVERED

You will:

Create a mental model of your plan for getting out of poverty.

Create a mental model for prosperity for the community.

WHY IT'S IMPORTANT

Mental models help us hold our plans in our mind so we can make good choices and monitor our progress.

A mental model of prosperity for the community makes us problem solvers in the community. We can contribute to a better life for everyone.

HOW IT'S CONNECTED TO YOU

We started this workbook by making a mental model of poverty, of what it's like to be stuck in the tyranny of survival.

The mental models we create now will be about taking responsibility for ourselves and for the community. We have the power to do something about our situations, and we can help solve problems in our systems that create poverty.

ACTIVITY

Activity: Creating a mental model for your personal path out of poverty
Time: 60 minutes
Materials: Worksheets and mental models
Procedure: 1) Look back over the mental models that you've created and think about how far you've come. Think about the future story you used to have and the future story that you are making.

2) Look at the plans you just made, the goals and action steps, the people who will support you, and the work that lies ahead.

3) Using these thoughts, think of a way to draw a mental model or write a story of the changes you are already making and are going to keep making.

4) Share your mental model with others. How many times have we found that building on each other's ideas helps to improve our thinking? Get ideas from theirs to use in your mental model.

DISCUSSION

1. When you think back over the investigations we've done, what things stand out as the most important for you?

2. When you think about what it took for you to create your own path out of poverty, what did you learn about yourself?

3. Where are you in relation to the stages of change now?

4. When was it that you became motivated to change?

5. What changes have you already made in the way you think and act?

In the space below, write or draw your thoughts and ideas about
completing your plans for building your resources.

REFLECTIONS REFLECTIONS REFLECTIONS REFLECTIONS REFLECTIONS

MENTAL MODEL FOR COMMUNITY PROSPERITY

Activity: Creating a mental model for community prosperity

Time: 45 minutes

Materials: Flip chart

Procedures: 1) Have a group discussion about the difference between taking responsibility for solving personal problems (such as taking action to build your own resources) and taking responsibility for community solutions to fight poverty. We've often said that poverty is about more than the choices of the poor. If we hold the community responsible for creating a wide range of strategies to fight poverty, then we can help the community do just that. Now that we are taking responsibility for our own choices, it's time to consider how we also can be problem solvers in the community.

2) Discuss what it means to have prosperity and economic security for all people. What would it take to have that happen? Think back over the information on the wealth gap and the research on poverty. What strategies are needed? How can we contribute to getting the community to work on those strategies?

3) Make a list of the ideas generated by the group.

4) Work on a mental model together.

5) Decide how to share this mental model and your ideas with the community.

DISCUSSION

1. Did the mental model for community prosperity include strategies from all four areas of research on the causes of poverty?

2. Has your attitude toward the community changed since beginning this workbook? If so, how?

3. Has your attitude toward the middle class changed? Toward the wealthy? If so, how?

4. How might we build partnerships with people from other economic classes?

5. How do you think of yourself differently now that you have contributed ideas for the betterment of the community?

In the space below, write or draw your thoughts, ideas,
and dreams about community prosperity.

REFLECTIONS REFLECTIONS REFLECTIONS REFLECTIONS REFLECTIONS

NEW NEW NEW NEW NEW **VOCABULARY** NEW NEW NEW NEW NEW

Words	Meanings

Closing and Transition

Throughout these weeks we've often asked, "Where are you in the stages of change?" One hopes we are all at the action stage now. It could be that you have already begun to take action – but, if not, this is the time to officially begin the action phase.

This is also a time to celebrate and to thank those who participated in the development of your plan. Take a few moments to thank each person.

Congratulations!
We know the mental models and plans you have made will work for you!

In the space below, express (through pictures or words or both)
how you're feeling right now.

REFLECTIONS REFLECTIONS **REFLECTIONS** REFLECTIONS REFLECTIONS

MODULE 14

Where to Go to Build Personal and Community Resources

Empowerment:
A Course in Personal Empowerment
2001 Twin Cities RISE!
800 Washington Ave. N., Suite 203
Minneapolis, MN 55401
(612) 338-0295
Build your emotional resources by taking this 15-week course with a facilitator.

National Community Reinvestment Coalition (NCRC)
733 15th St., NW, Suite 540
Washington, DC 20005
(202) 628-8866
www.ncrc.org/cra/how2usecra.html
Here is information on how to work with your local banks to provide services to all sectors of the community.

Professional Development and Its Practical Applications
Designed and developed by Optimal Employment & Consulting
31 E. First St., Dayton, OH 45402
(937) 223-8084
This is a student-friendly, organized approach to the world of job hunting, résumé writing, interviewing, and personal skill development.

Realizing the American Dream:
A Workbook for Homebuyers
Kevin McQueen, Deborah Schneider and Alison Thresher, First Edition; Laurie Maggiano, Second Edition
Neighborhood Reinvestment Corporation
1325 G St., NW, Suite 800
Washington, DC 20005-3100
(202) 376-2400
(800) 438-5547
www.nw.org   nrti@nw.org
This workbook has all the information a person could need to buy a house.

Wisconsin Literacy
Wisconsin Technical College System
310 Price Place
P.O. Box 7874
Madison, WI 53707-7874
www.board.tec.wi.us

Anti-Predatory Lending Toolkit
National Community Reinvestment Coalition
  (NCRC)
733 15th St., NW, Suite 540
Washington, DC 20005
(202) 628-8866
www.NCRC.org

**Building Communities from the Inside Out:
  A Path Toward Finding and Mobilizing a
  Community's Assets**
John P. Kretzmann, John L. McKnight
The Asset-Based Community Development
  Institute
ACTA Publications
4848 N. Clark St.
Chicago, IL 60640
(800) 397-2282
www.northwestern.edu/ipr/people/mcknight.html

Economic Policy Institute
Research and Ideas for Working People
www.epinet.org
**Here is information on living wage ordinances,
minimum wage, budgets, retirement security,
Social Security, unemployment, and insurance.**

**The Growing Divide: Inequality and the Roots
  of Economic Insecurity**
United for a Fair Economy
37 Temple Place, Second Floor
Boston, MA 02111
(617) 423-2148
info@faireconomy.org
www.faireconomy.org

Websites

Wages, Jobs, Housing, Hunger, and Community Action

www.acorn.org
*ACORN (Association for Community
  Organizing for Reform Now)*
United States' largest community organization
of low- and moderate-income families: information on predatory lending, affordable housing,
living wage, community reinvestment, utilities.

www.bettercommunities.org
Building Better Communities Network
Clearinghouse for building inclusive communities
and affordable housing.

www.dosomething.org
Do Something
For young people who want to take community
action.

www.jwj.org
Jobs with Justice
Improving working people's standard of living,
Jobs with Justice is in 40 cities in 29 states.

www.nicwj.org
*National Interfaith Community for Worker
  Justice*
Information on wages, childcare, etc.

www.hlihc.org
National Low Income Housing Coalition
Dedicated to ending America's affordable
housing crisis. Information on all related topics.

Wages, Jobs, Housing, Hunger, and Community Action *(continued)*

www.oxfamamerica.org
Oxfam America
Long-term solutions to poverty, hunger, social injustice; elimination of root causes of social and economic inequalities by challenging structural barriers.

www.ufenet.org
United for a Fair Economy
United for a Fair Economy is a national, independent, nonpartisan, 501(c)(3) non-profit organization. UFE raises awareness that concentrated wealth and power undermine the economy, corrupt democracy, deepen the racial divide, and tear communities apart. UFE supports and helps build social movements for greater equality.

www.welfareinfo.org
Welfare Information Network
Research and articles on poverty issues.

www.wihed.org
Women's Institute for Housing and Economic Development
Developing innovative real estate projects and supportive communities that work for low-income women and their families.

www.nw.org
Neighborhood Works, Neighborhood Reinvestment Corporation
Revitalizing older urban neighborhoods by mobilizing public, private, and community resources at the neighborhood level.

Building Resources

www.globalethics.org
Institute of Global Ethics
Building integrity and ethical decision making. Offers training and curriculum.

www.microenterpriseworks.org
Association of Enterprise Opportunities
Information promoting enterprise opportunities for people with limited access.

www.ncrc.org
National Community Reinvestment Coalition
Strategies that promote access to credit and capital, information about the Community Reinvestment Act, Financial Literacy campaigns, predators, etc.

www.philosophyofliving.com
Psychology of Mind, Health Realization
Building cognitive and emotional resources.

www.resiliency.com/htm/contents.htm
Resiliency In Action
Resiliency resources for young people.

www.thrivenet.com
Thrivenet
Information and links about resiliency, becoming stronger through extreme adversity.

Reading List

Alexie, Sherman. (1993).
The Lone Ranger and Tonto Fistfight in Heaven.
New York, NY: HarperPerennial.

Bragg, Rick. (1998).
All Over but the Shoutin'.
New York, NY: Vintage Books.

Brouwer, Steve. (1998).
Sharing the Pie: A Citizen's Guide to Wealth and Power in America.
New York, NY: Henry Holt & Company, Inc.

Galeano, Eduardo. (1998).
Upside Down: A Primer for the Looking-Glass World.
New York, NY: Metropolitan Books.

Hart, Betty, & Risley, Todd. (1995).
Meaningful Differences in the Everyday Experience of Young American Children.
Baltimore, MD: Paul H. Brookes Publishing Co.

Hooks, Bell. (2000).
Where We Stand: Class Matters.
New York, NY: Routledge.

O'Connor, Alice. (2001).
Poverty Knowledge: Social Science, Social Policy, and the Poor in Twentieth-Century U.S. History.
Princeton, NJ: Princeton University Press.

Phillips, Kevin. (2002).
Wealth and Democracy: A Political History of the American Rich.
New York, NY: Broadway Books.

Putnam, Robert D. (2000).
Bowling Alone: The Collapse and Revival of American Community.
New York, NY: Simon & Schuster.

Upchurch, Carl. (1996).
Convicted in the Womb.
New York, NY: Bantam Books.

Process, Inc.

www.ahaprocess.com
PO Box 727, Highlands, TX 77562-0727
(800) 424-9484; fax: (281) 426-8705
store@ahaprocess.com

ORDER FORM

UPS SHIP TO ADDRESS: (no post office boxes, please)

NAME: _____ E-mail _____

ORGANIZATION: _____

ADDRESS: _____

CITY/STATE/ZIP: _____

TELEPHONE: _____ FAX: _____

QTY	TITLE	1-4 Copies	5+ Copies	Total
	A Framework for Understanding Poverty	22.00	15.00	
	Understanding Learning	10.00	7.00	
	A Framework for Understanding Poverty Workbook	7.00	7.00	
	Learning Structures Workbook	7.00	7.00	
	A Framework for Understanding Poverty Audio Workshop Kit (includes Day 1 & 2 audiotapes – 10 – and 4 books listed above) **S/H: $10.50**	225.00	225.00	
	Un Marco Para Entender La Pobreza	22.00	15.00	
	Putting the Pieces Together (replaces Application of Learning Structures)	10.00	10.00	
	Daily Math Practice for Virginia SOLs – Grade 4	22.00	15.00	
	Mr. Base Ten Invents Mathematics	22.00	15.00	
	Think Rather of Zebra	18.00	15.00	
	Berrytales – Plays in One Act	25.00	20.00	
	What Every Church Member Should Know About Poverty	22.00	15.00	
	A Picture Is Worth a Thousand Words	18.00	15.00	
	Parenting Someone Else's Child: The Foster Parents' How-To Manual	22.00	15.00	
	Bridges Out of Poverty: Strategies for Professionals & Communities	22.00	15.00	
	Removing the Mask: Giftedness in Poverty	25.00	20.00	
	Environmental Opportunity Profile (25/set-incl 1 FAQ)	25.00	25.00	
	Addit'l FAQs Environmental Opportunities Profile manual	3.00	3.00	
	Slocumb-Payne Teacher Perception Inventory (25/set)	25.00	25.00	
	Living on a Tightrope: A Survival Handbook for Principals	22.00	15.00	
	Hidden Rules of Class at Work	22.00	15.00	
	Hear Our Cry: Boys in Crisis	22.00	15.00	
	Tucker Signing Strategies Video & Manual **S/H: $8.50**	125.00	125.00	
	Tucker Signs Reference Cards on CD	25.00	25.00	
	Take-Home Books for Tucker Signing Strategies for Reading	22.00	15.00	
	Preventing School Violence – 5 videos & manual **S/H: $15.00**	995.00	995.00	
	Preventing School Violence CD – PowerPoint presentation	25.00	25.00	
	Preventing School Violence Training Manual	15.00	15.00	
	Audiotapes, What Every Church Member Should Know About Poverty	25.00	25.00	
	Meeting Standards & Raising Test Scores When You Don't Have Much Time or Money (4 videos/training manual) **S/H: $15.00**	995.00	995.00	
	Meeting Standards & Raising Test Scores Training Manual	18.00	18.00	
	Meeting Standards & Raising Test Scores Resource Manual	18.00	18.00	
	Meeting Standards & Raising Test Scores CD – PowerPoint presentation	50.00	50.00	
	Rita's Stories (2 videos) **S/H: $8.50**	150.00	150.00	
	Ruby Payne Video Sampler	10.00	10.00	
	aha! 12 oz. mugs (white with red logo and website)	8.00	2 @ 15.00	
	Rubygems! 16-month calendar – Ideas for working with parents $2 S/H	10.00	5.00	

For Certified Trainers Only – Please note date/city of training:

	A Framework for Understanding Poverty Video Sets (12 videos) (Day 1 & Day 2 of Framework seminar) Circle one: VHS or DVD **S/H: $25.00**	1995.00	1995.00	
	A Framework for Understanding Poverty CD – PowerPoint presentation	50.00	50.00	
	A Framework for Understanding Poverty CD – Enhanced PowerPoint pres.	100.00	100.00	
	Bridges Out of Poverty CD – PowerPoint presentation	50.00	50.00	

Total Quantity	Subtotal	
	S/H	
	Tax	
	Total	

S/H: 1-4 books – $4.50 plus $2.00 each additional book up to 4 books, [1 calendar $2]

5+ books – 8% of total, *(special S/H for videos). E-mail for international rates.*

TAX: 8.25% Texas residents only

Please follow these terms when ordering. Prices subject to change.

AmEx   MC   Visa   Discover

CREDIT CARD # _____ EXP. DATE_____Signature_____

AUTHORIZATION # _____ PO # _____ (please fax PO with order) Check # _____.

Please see website for all current offerings